BASS LESSON GOLDMINE

AUDIO
ACCESS
INCLUDED

100 JAZZ LESSONS

BY JOSH NEEDLEMAN & MATT RYBICKI

To access audio visit:
www.halleonard.com/mylibrary

Enter Code
8648-2996-4228-0127

ISBN 978-1-4803-9844-3

HAL•LEONARD®
CORPORATION

7777 W. BLUEMOUND RD. P.O. BOX 13819 MILWAUKEE, WI 53213

In Australia Contact:
Hal Leonard Australia Pty. Ltd.
4 Lentara Court
Cheltenham, Victoria, 3192 Australia
Email: ausadmin@halleonard.com.au

Visit Hal Leonard Online at
www.halleonard.com

CONTENTS

Lessons 1–50 by Matt Rybicki

Lessons 51–100 by Josh Needleman

PROPER HAND PLACEMENT: PLUCKING HAND

The plucking hand is probably the most influential element for manipulating timbre while playing the bass. Different techniques enable the sound to be warmer or more percussive, the bassist to play slap style, or for the upright player to play with the bow. There are not only a wide range of hand positions for basic execution, but even more possibilities within each technique, as bassists have developed special ways to approach the basic skills over the years.

Here are a variety of photos that show conventional approaches to using the plucking hand:

One finger for percussive, higher-volume playing

One finger for a softer or warmer sound

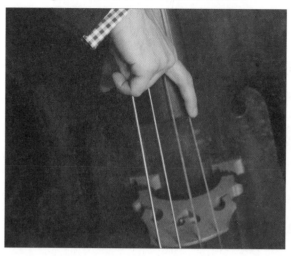

Typical position of the thumb

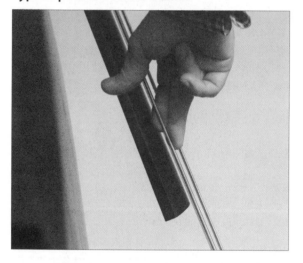

Two fingers together

Alternating two fingers

Alternate one-finger technique

Hand position for slap technique

German bow hold

Typical position of the thumb

Position for a warmer, rounder sound

French bow hold

Conventional electric bass technique

Position for a more percussive sound

Hand position for slap technique

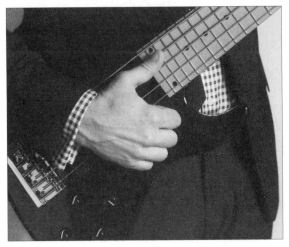

LESSON #2: ONE-FINGER WARMUP

In order to use the first finger of our plucking hand effectively, it is very helpful to isolate it via various exercises. This series of examples illustrates how simple, repetitive movements of one finger can greatly increase our independence and strength. The benefits of this particular technique are that we achieve the biggest possible sound while still allowing for flexibility and fluidity with the plucking hand in general.

While there are a variety of plucking-hand finger techniques, each with its own purpose, this exercise serves as an anchor for the other techniques because it emphasizes finger, hand, and wrist control, body- and arm-weight use, and disciplined focus on strength-building for each finger.

Find a full-length mirror and place it in a location where you can watch yourself play. You want to observe your hand placement and shape, along with listening to yourself and concentrating on steady time, an even sound, and slight exertion. If your muscles hurt, stop and rest. Unfortunately, it is nearly impossible to avoid skin abrasions and blisters as you work toward creating permanent callouses. If you are experiencing pain, use your best judgment and seek out the advice of your teacher to determine whether to rest or to play.

Set your metronome to 60 beats per minute (bpm) and simply play whole notes on the open strings, paying close attention to your hand placement, sound, projection, and rhythm. Take notice of your body placement, your arm position, and the rigidity of your wrists, forearms, and thumb. The body should be relaxed but upright. Arms, wrists, and forearms are also engaged but relaxed. Try to experiment with using the *weight* of your arm itself to create force to pull the string. Let gravity do some of the work for you. The thumb should rest on the side of the fingerboard on upright and on top of the pickup for electric. On the double bass, the end of the index finger should be at the end of the fingerboard and the remaining fingers should be curled up into your palm. To facilitate this, you may want to place a small paperclip (or something similar) in your hand and hold it with your middle, ring, and pinky fingers. This will prevent your hand from opening up while you play. After this, increase the rhythmic value to half notes, making sure to maintain posture, position, sound, and rhythm.

EXAMPLE 1

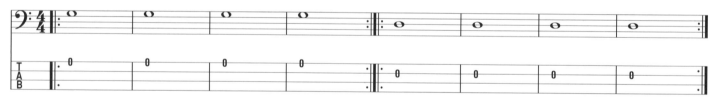

EXAMPLE 2

Now play quarter notes and eighth notes, and continue on your own with eighth-note triplets and 16th notes (not shown).

EXAMPLE 3

As you increase in tempo or note subdivision, you will naturally need a lighter touch to execute rhythms in time. This is normal and should be embraced. Strive for the biggest sound possible, even while playing fast.

To push the muscles even further, wrap a small hand towel (or something similar) fully around the neck of the instrument so that no notes ring out. Then, practice the same exercises from above. You'll notice that without the strings' natural momentum, striking with the pluck hand becomes more difficult. Maintain the intensity of working for a loud and full sound, even though no notes are being heard. At the end of the exercises, you'll be surprised how much easier playing open strings will be.

LESSON #3:

PROPER HAND PLACEMENT: FRETTING HAND

If we use good form with our fretting hand, we will have more stamina, avoid injury, and be free to have the dexterity to execute musical ideas. The types of techniques here are smaller in number, but no less important for playing the bass well.

Finger shape on fingerboard

Thumb location behind the neck

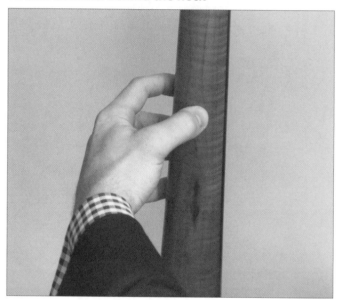

Alternate view of proper hand shape

Thumb position on upright

Fretting-hand position for double stop

Fretting-hand shape for playing an octave

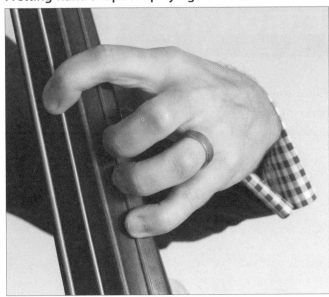

Electric fretting-hand shape

Electric thumb location

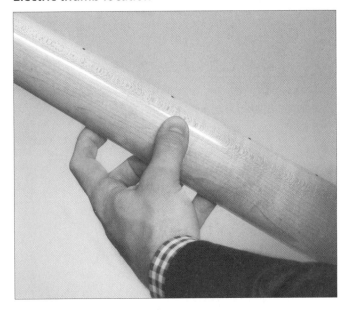

Electric fretting-hand position for chords and double stops

Electric fretting-hand shape for playing an octave

LESSON #4: FRETTING-HAND WORKOUT

The strength of our non-plucking (i.e., fretting) hand is often overlooked as we develop our bass-playing skills. However, this hand is critically important with respect to creating a good sound, building dexterity, and maintaining stamina while playing. Additionally, as we strengthen our muscles, we help to prevent injury and overall pain that can occur from a lifetime of playing the bass.

These exercises are meant to address strength and stamina specifically, but will also help with overall facility, fingerboard knowledge, intonation on the upright bass, and time. The primary goal here, though, is to focus on the ergonomic aspects of playing the instrument. These exercises are not intended to be melodic or musical; they're simply a muscle exercise with powerful results if practiced regularly.

Broadly speaking, we will spend a set amount of time in each fingerboard position, shifting by half steps at the end of each time interval. Starting at the half-position, we slowly work towards thumb position and then back down. Set your metronome to 72 bpm. For upright, use triplets in half-position, and for electric, use 16th notes, each for 30 seconds. Start with a basic 1–2–4 fingering for upright and 1–2–3–4 for electric, crossing all the strings while ascending and descending.

EXAMPLE 1

At the end of those 30 seconds, shift up a half step to second position and repeat the fingering and rhythms for the next 30 seconds. You should strive for accuracy in your hand placement and rhythmic stability throughout the whole exercise. There are many options for keeping track of your timing intervals. A digital watch with seconds displayed or an app for your smartphone will do the trick.

EXAMPLE 2

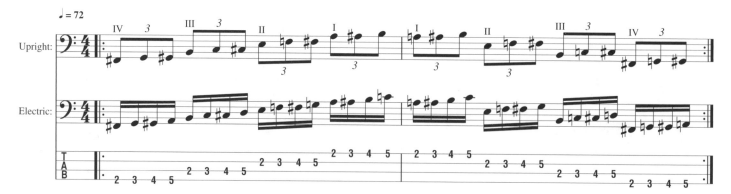

Continue this process until you reach thumb position and then work backwards, one fingerboard position at a time. Remember to spend 30 seconds in each position as you move back towards your starting point.

These exercises will be difficult on your hand, and you absolutely should stop if you experience pain, similar to lifting weights in a gym. It is very common to have to stop for a minute or so about halfway through the ascending and/or descending portions. If you need to, shorten the interval of time to 15 seconds so you can experience some progress. Do work towards 30 seconds per position, though.

To add interest and complexity to the exercises, experiment with different fingerings while in a given position.

EXAMPLE 3

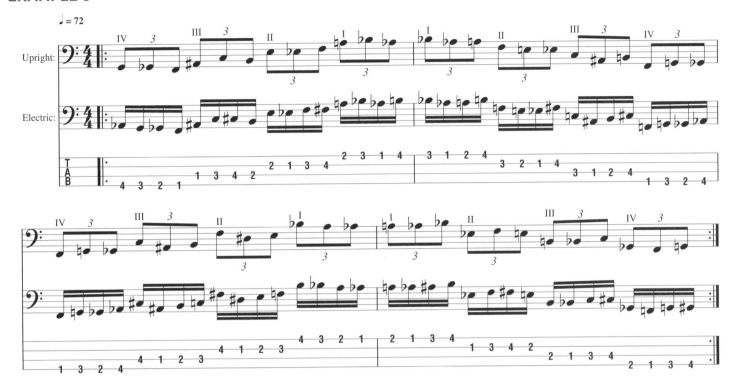

Now, for a greater challenge, we'll add the element of alternate string-crossing.

EXAMPLE 4

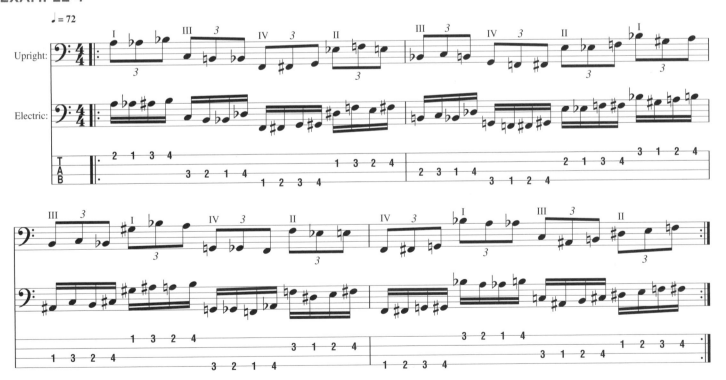

With patience and discipline, this exercise will provide a real sense of strength, comfort with the instrument, and much greater endurance for both practice and performance.

LESSON #5: STRING CROSSING

When deconstructing the various elements of physically playing the bass, string crossing is a simple but important skill to master and maintain. The more we focus on becoming highly efficient and nimble while moving from string to string, the more we are able to instinctively know the feel of the instrument and succeed in delivering the musical statements that we are striving for.

Begin with open strings. Take your time and pay attention to how your fingers move from string to string, working to maintain a consistent sound and rhythm. Set your metronome at 60–72 bpm to start and, as with all exercises, find your own variations in order to challenge yourself and expand your abilities.

Vary the pattern below, starting and ending on different open strings. The idea is to explore the many possibilities that you may encounter in performance and feel comfortable with *any* movement from one string to another.

EXAMPLE 1

Begin to increase the velocity of rhythms at the same tempo. Then, mix up the patterns of open strings and find your own options.

EXAMPLE 2

Now focus on repeating specific string-to-string movements to isolate and strengthen any weak areas. Again, create your own variations of the example here in order to maximize your progress.

EXAMPLE 3

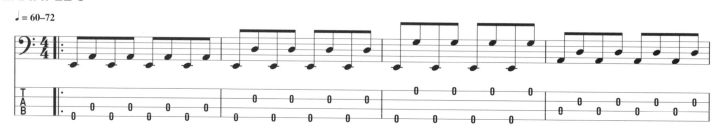

Next, begin to incorporate the fretting hand, utilizing intervals across strings.

EXAMPLE 4

Lastly, try simple triadic patterns that enable you to play across all of the strings.

EXAMPLE 5

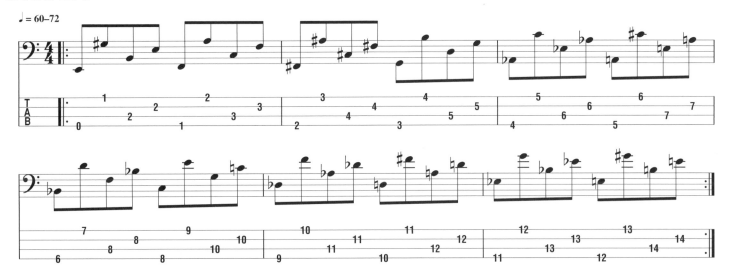

LESSON #6: FRETTING-HAND INDEPENDENCE

There are many exercises for improving our plucking hand, but in my experience, few focus exclusively on the fretting hand. Usually, fretting-hand work involves the plucking hand as well. Below are some exercises that focus solely on the fretting hand. I've found them to be very rewarding!

Pluck the open strings with each finger of your *fretting* hand. You can experiment with different locations on the neck, but spend time playing the exercise in a given position. Your hand will naturally gravitate toward proper technique. Take notice of how far your fingers travel from the string and do your best to improve the fine motor skills involved in keeping them as close to the fingerboard as possible.

EXAMPLE 1

Utilize slurs (hammer-ons and pull-offs) to strengthen your hand. Remember: here, you aren't plucking the string with your plucking hand, but rather doing your best to create volume with your fretting hand. As always, find and develop your own extensions of these drills to increase your skill.

EXAMPLE 2

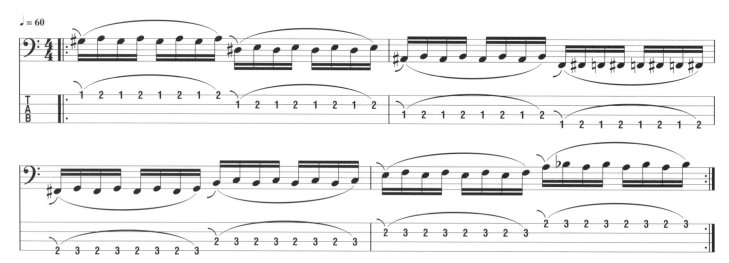

Now target the movements involved in moving from one note to another. As with any kind of shifting on the bass, properly preparing to carry through from one position to another is critical to playing efficiently.

EXAMPLE 3

*Leave finger down as long as possible from note to note.

This exercise is similar to Example 1, but involves actually fretting notes on the fingerboard. Still using only your fretting hand, alternate plucking the string with placing your fingers down and sounding out a note. The fingering will differ here between upright and electric, as the upright doesn't involve the ring finger until you are in thumb position.

EXAMPLE 4

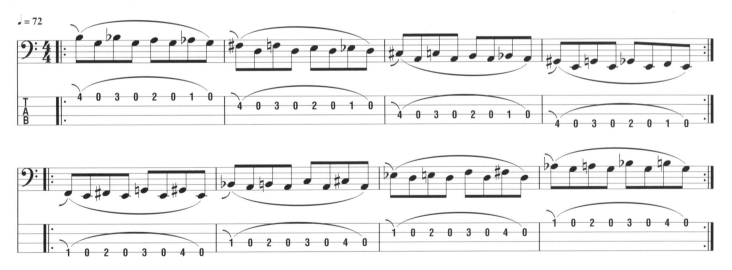

LESSON #7: TWO-FINGER WARMUP

This lesson uses simple parameters to bring attention to an important rudimentary ability: playing with both the first and the second fingers of our plucking hand. Adding the second plucking finger greatly increases the variety of pattern combinations to practice and enables us to perform a wider range of musical phrases.

In Example 1, use open strings and increase rhythmic value over the length of the drill. Practice on all open strings.

EXAMPLE 1

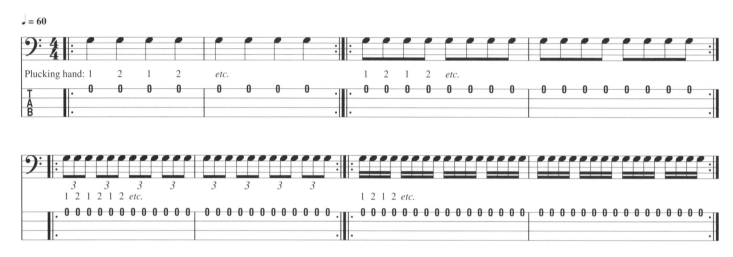

Next, incorporate alternate plucking combinations.

EXAMPLE 2

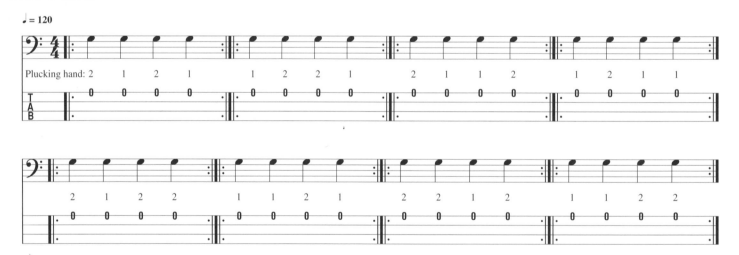

Now add string crossing into the mix while still using open strings.

EXAMPLE 3

Lastly, use alternate fingerings while crossing strings.

EXAMPLE 4

LESSON #8: HAND SYNCHRONICITY

Using our plucking and fretting hands in tandem is important to successfully implement our musical ideas. If the hands are not in sync, we can stumble with timing and rhythm and our phrases can sound disjointed or sloppy. Use these exercises to enhance your coordination between the two.

Using a metronome, play repetitive half steps chromatically, ensuring that your fretting fingers match the precise rhythm of your plucking fingers.

EXAMPLE 1

Now do the same with whole steps and minor 3rds.

EXAMPLE 2

Shifting from string to string can be one place where our hands become slightly separated. Use this exercise to find the most efficient motion for moving from one string to another.

EXAMPLE 3

Shifting positions can also make it difficult to keep the hands in sync.

EXAMPLE 4

*Upright string numerals

Lastly, combine these common places where time is lost into a more advanced exercise.

EXAMPLE 5

LESSON #9: TARGET PRACTICE

Music, in its best form, is naturally unpredictable. Melodic lines and phrases often require dramatic shifts on the fingerboard, and we need to be confident in our ability to make those shifts. As the great jazz bassist Ray Brown once told me about playing the bass: "If you hesitate, you're dead." The exercises below, when practiced regularly and diligently, should aid in removing any hesitation. Additionally, for the double bass, these examples will work wonders for improving intonation.

The basic idea is to simply repeat intervals accurately and in time while using different fretting-hand fingerings. Because fingerings are decided in the context of what comes before and after a given note, we want to explore various options and become as comfortable as possible with them. (**Note:** Fingerings will differ between upright and electric bass.)

Practice these exercises slowly with a metronome, and work for economy of motion, as well as for good sound, timing, and accuracy. There are quite a few more fingering combinations than listed here—and you should explore them all—but start with whole steps, minor 3rds, major 3rds, and perfect 4ths.

EXAMPLE 1

Next, add tritones (diminished 5ths), perfect 5ths, minor 6ths, and major 6ths.

EXAMPLE 2

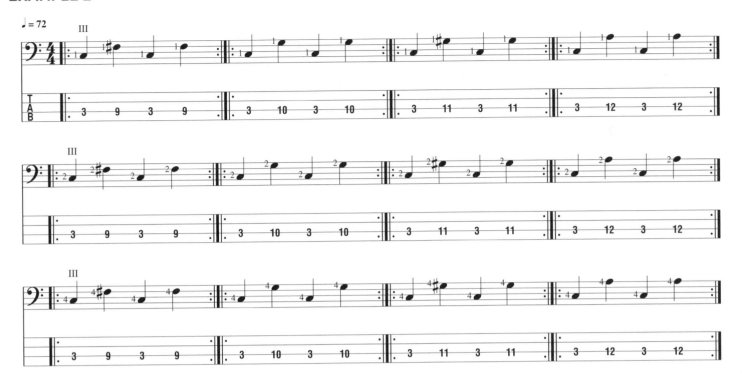

Finally, add minor and major 7ths, octaves, and major 9ths.

EXAMPLE 3

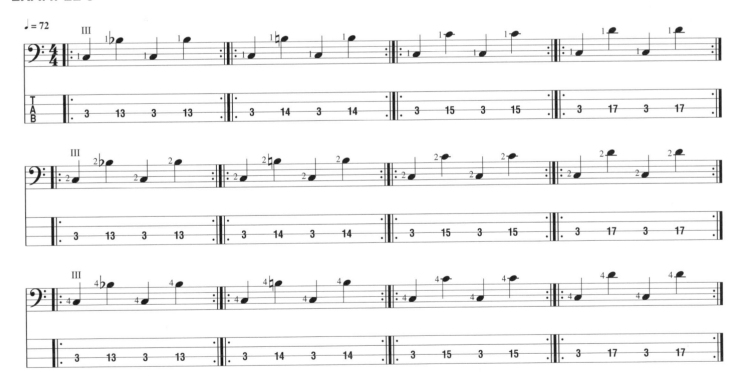

For a full workout, you can implement the same ideas for larger intervals and intervals that cross strings.

INTONATION WITH A DRONE

While this lesson is geared towards the upright bassist, electric players can use it as well. By using a repetitive single note that we know is in tune, we can investigate and hone our intonation on the upright. For electric players, this will benefit your technique and can be an exercise for hearing intervals against a fixed pitch.

This exercise works best when playing arco, as the bow enables us to hear the pitch very clearly. As usual with fundamental drills, go slowly, use a metronome, and listen carefully.

Begin with the consonant intervals of a perfect 5th and an octave and use an open string as the drone. Be sure to practice the same idea and the same series of intervals with all of the open strings.

EXAMPLE 1

Next, use more extended or dissonant intervals like tritones, 6ths, and 7ths.

EXAMPLE 2

Now use a fretted pitch, one that you can confidently play in tune. Check that pitch regularly against a related open string (for example, use the open G string to check a fretted C). Use the same series of intervals against that fretted, fixed note.

EXAMPLE 3

LESSON #11: DOUBLE STOPS

One way to add color to bass lines or solos is the technique of playing more than one note at a time. Double stops can provide weight to a repeated note or pattern, as well as add depth to our musical statements. Ultimately, the goal is to have many tools available to express ourselves musically, and this is one surefire skill to keep in our repertoire.

The most basic double stop is a root and perfect 5th. As mentioned above, when played simultaneously, these notes can add "heft" to the sound of the root. I've found this particularly effective when performing a single-chord vamp or within a song with many measures of the same chord (e.g., Duke Ellington's "Caravan").

In this first exercise, familiarize yourself with the sound and feel of this double stop across the range of the fingerboard. As always, the fingerings for electric and upright bass will differ.

EXAMPLE 1

Another useful set of intervals are major and minor 3rds and perfect 4ths. As is often the case, these intervals are particularly effective higher on the neck, as our ears can process the notes a bit more clearly. Study these exercises until you not only feel comfortable playing them, but can expand them to include a variety of rhythms.

EXAMPLE 2

So far, we have examined double stops that are located on adjacent strings. Here are several other intervals on non-adjacent strings that you should investigate and put into a practice regimen that includes multiple rhythms, tempos, variations in sequence, and style. In short, take these simple examples and create your own series of drills.

EXAMPLE 3

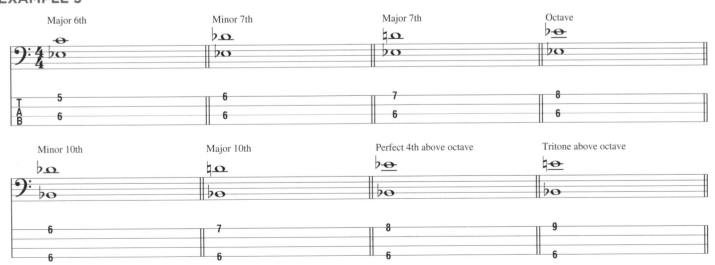

LESSON #12: FINGERING STRATEGIES

When playing any instrument, economizing the movement of our hands and fingers requires intelligent choices. However, we often reach a certain point in our fingering progress and plateau there. This lesson contains some basic ideas, reminders, and examples of clever or logical fingering choices that should help to inspire new ideas or work you through problem areas.

The first reminder is that decisions on how to play a given passage are purely based on the *context* in which that passage appears. We should always be asking ourselves this: "Where is the note or phrase coming from, and where is it headed?" For example, let's look at the various fingering choices in Example 1. Notice that the order of the fingers used will change substantially according to the notes that precede and follow the four-note "cell" (the notes we approach and leave in various ways). Also note that there are differences between the two staves in this lesson: the top staff relates fingerings based on upright bass, while the bottom tab staff is geared toward electric.

EXAMPLE 1

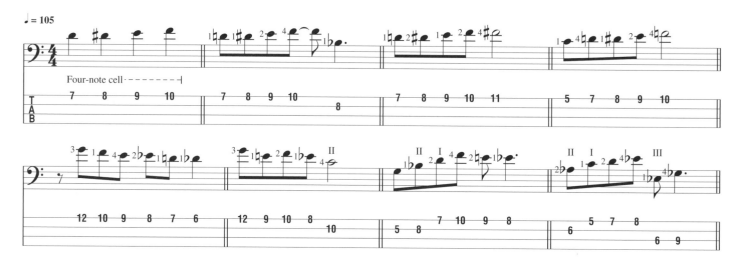

For fast passages, one clever option for making large position shifts is to incorporate an open string into the phrase. Playing the open string gives us just enough time to make a big shift up or down the fingerboard and has the added benefits of being played at its full rhythmic value and offering a quick reference for our ears to ensure that we are playing in tune.

EXAMPLE 2

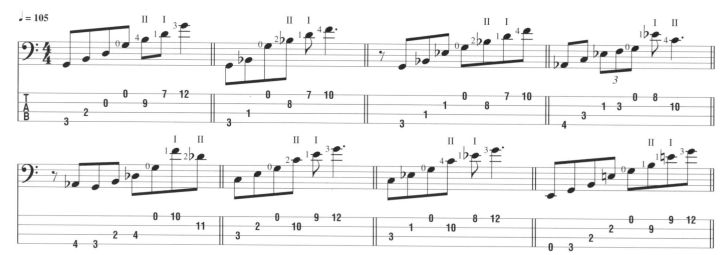

Most often, we are taught to play diatonic scales with two or three notes per string. While this allows for learning the fingerboard across the strings and accessing these notes within one position, it can box us in and create unnecessary or awkward shifts. We can become mentally boxed in, as well, with fewer options quickly available to our fingers. Try to practice your scales with logical position shifts within the scale. This will expand your comfort with the neck and provide the freedom to go various directions while improvising.

EXAMPLE 3

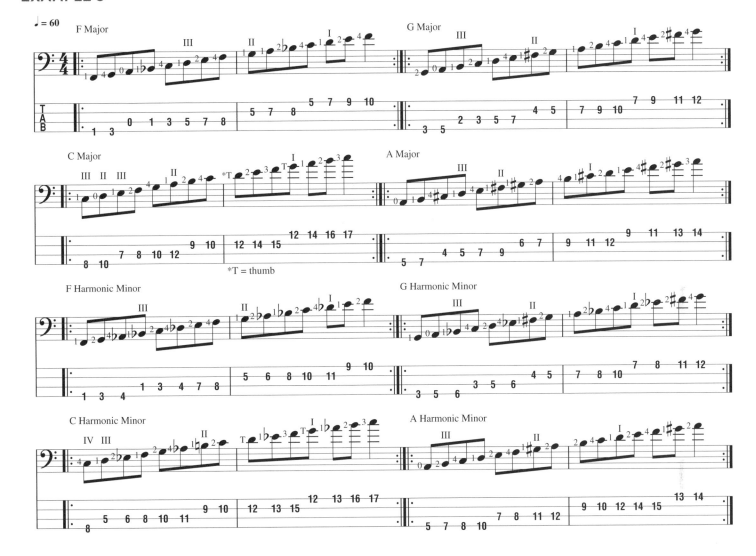

As an instrument, unamplified upright bass is generally soft in volume. In early jazz, bassists such as Pops Foster, John Lindsay, Slam Stewart, and Milt Hinton developed a style that incorporated percussive slapping and pulling of the strings for more volume and to further define the rhythm when no drummer was present. This technique has been used, refined, and built upon, especially by electric players. Verdine White, Larry Graham, Louis Johnson, and Stanley Clarke are some of the bassists who brought electric bass slapping to new levels in the '60s and '70s. While slapping is primarily used in funk, gospel, and R&B today on the electric bass, and generally relegated to novelty status on the upright, I feel strongly that we have a duty to study and understand the lineage of bass playing. For this reason, we should become familiar with the technique, at least on a fundamental level.

If you have never experimented with slapping before, here is a very simple exercise that coordinates both the slap and the pluck, or "pop." On the upright, the plucking hand strikes the fingerboard primarily with a relaxed fist and index finger, or on the side of the first finger, depending on the phrase. Plucking ("popping" on electric bass) is achieved by pulling the string away from the fingerboard, instead of across it. On electric, the "slapping" part is created by the thumb striking the end of the fingerboard.

EXAMPLE 1

Besides adding variety to the timbre of the bass, slapping enables us to make fast interval jumps, as our plucking hand is positioned across multiple strings, instead of just one. To investigate how your hands negotiate the strings with slap technique, try this musical line:

EXAMPLE 2

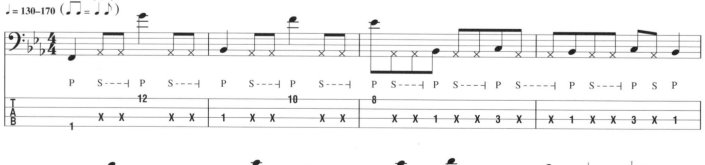

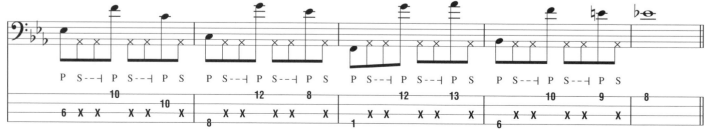

An effective use of the slapping technique is to ornament melodic phrases with the percussive slaps. In Example 3A, notice how the plucked notes create a melody centered on an E♭ major scale. This is punctuated by syncopated slapping that creates color and interest. Example 3B has a very clearly defined A diminished arpeggio that is made more compelling by the rhythms in between.

EXAMPLES 3A-B

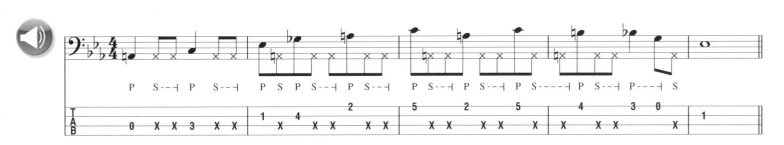

So far, we've looked at phrases that tend to go back and forth between just two strings. Here is a relatively basic one-position phrase whose slapping technique is more "musical."

EXAMPLE 4

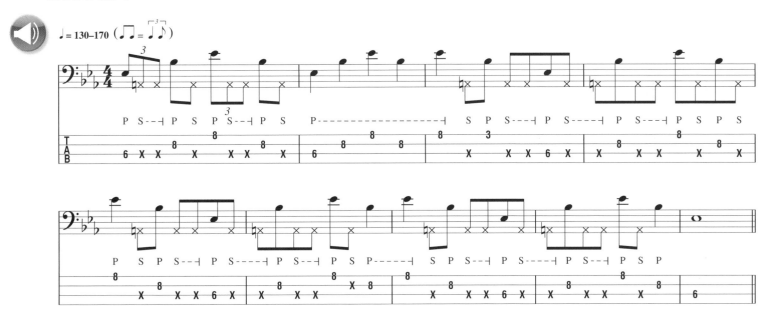

RAKING STRINGS

To add movement and interest to a line or solo phrase, the technique of "raking" across the strings is a good option to have in our vocabulary. It's a simple concept and very effective when used properly. Raking fills space between very large interval jumps when moving from high to low, helps to execute triplet "drops," and generally gives a sense of propulsion to the time. Primarily a percussive effect, the string rakes can also be applied to fretted passages where appropriate.

The technique is created by simply striking strings from high to low (generally starting from the G string) in quick succession with only one finger of your plucking hand. So, rather than playing each string individually, your plucking hand moves in one motion while your fretting fingers make contact with the strings, one right after the other. In certain phrases, the final note of the rake may be slurred from the last open string played. Use this first exercise to familiarize yourself with the concept and to build comfort with the movement.

EXAMPLE 1

As mentioned, raking strings is useful when making a large interval jump from high to low. Here are some examples that you can play through to understand the idea. Remember that the rake should be played in rhythm and in such a way that you aid in the forward movement of the time. Getting stuck on this effect can cause you to drag or otherwise negatively affect the pulse.

EXAMPLES 2A-D

Raking strings is a great way to perform effective triplet drops. These follow the same principle as large interval leaps—that is, keeping the time moving forward—but tend to involve more fretted notes and less of a percussive sound.

EXAMPLE 3

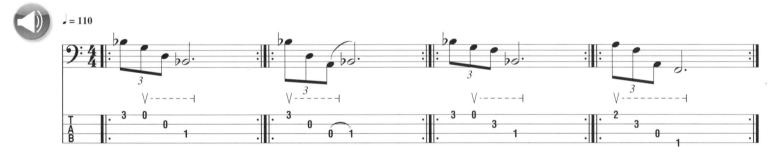

Here are some phrases that you might play in a solo or a bass fill while accompanying another instrument. The string rakes help make playing these kinds of musical statements easier.

EXAMPLE 4

LESSON #15: SOUND AND PROJECTION

The first thing that a listener hears when we are performing is our sound. No matter how musically experienced they are, any listener can process the quality of the sound that we project with our instrument. I believe that, for the upright bass, we should understand and put time into learning about a traditionally "good" sound. While this is ultimately subjective, the more that we understand about the physics of the instrument, the history of how it was played, and the skills necessary to create a big and warm sound, the better off we are as bassists. By learning our instrument in as much detail as possible, we can achieve confidence and freedom when we are creating our own musical moments.

Both upright and electric bassists have a wide variety of electronic gear to enhance, manipulate, and boost their sound. Ideally, these should be used to *support* the natural sound that we work to get from our instruments. Special effects, processors, and amplifiers in general are great tools to help us express our musical visions, but I feel that they should be applied after we have mastered the natural, organic approach to the bass.

Perhaps the most critical aspect of creating and perfecting our sound is nurturing and maintaining the sound that we want in our inner ear. We need a strong internal idea of the timbre, volume, length of notes, and so on that we want to produce before we can do so. The way to do this is to listen, and then listen some more. Recordings provide a great source of information for bass sounds, especially if we are studying a variety of approaches and sound concepts. However, to truly understand what the bass can—and perhaps *should*—sound like, we need to experience master bassists in live settings. The more we hear great bass players in performance, rehearsal, and (hopefully) private lessons, the more we are able to solidify a good sound in our inner ear. When you regularly pay attention to the sound of a bass played live, you begin to understand what is possible and reasonable, what works well when playing with others, and what kind of sound you are naturally drawn to. However, don't limit yourself to players to whom you gravitate; you may find more information from and an affinity for differing styles from a variety of players.

Some words that might describe a traditionally high-quality bass sound are "big," "warm," or "fat." Additionally, "growling," "punchy," or "hump" may also be used to describe other elements of the sound. To achieve these characteristics, both the plucking hand and the fretting hand come into play. The fretting hand fingers should be curved and touch the string with the meat of the fingertips. With the double bass, use the weight of your arm and let gravity help you place weight upon the fingerboard, rather than gripping the neck exclusively with your hand muscles.

 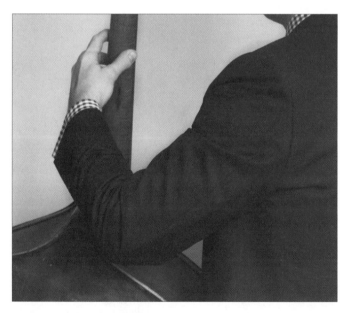

You have more timbral options with your plucking hand. The broad idea is that no matter the plucking-hand shape or position, you should strive to keep as much "meat" of your finger(s) on the string. With more surface area on the string, you'll produce a louder and bigger sound. On the upright bass, practice playing with your index finger parallel to the string, pulling the string towards you as if you were drawing back an arrow in a bow. For electric, your index finger will be almost perpendicular to the string, while allowing for a slight angle to accommodate a difference in first or second fingers. This is most effective when your other fingers are closed into your palm. Hold a small object in your remaining three fingers to keep your technique disciplined.

Using two fingers simultaneously is more common with the upright than the electric bass. However, when you alternate two fingers on either instrument, keep as much of your finger on the string as possible while still being able to maneuver through a phrase.

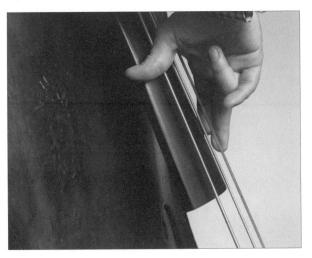
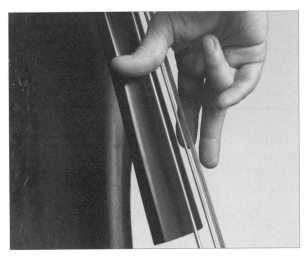

Effective projection of our sound is crucial to being heard. Some listeners have difficulty hearing and processing the low frequencies of the bass, since they rarely spend time focusing on the instrument as much as we, the players, do. We need to learn how to project the sound that we are ultimately hearing in our inner ear so that other band members and the audience can receive what we are offering. Volume, in and of itself, is an important factor in projection, but it is not the only ingredient in its makeup. Projecting our sound involves:

▶ A clear idea of the sound we want to express

▶ The technical aspects of creating that sound on the instrument

▶ Volume, or "fullness," of the notes that we are creating

▶ Clarity of ideas

▶ Accuracy of intonation

▶ Command of rhythm

▶ Facility on the instrument to execute a given statement

▶ Confidence in our musical intention

A slightly unconventional approach to refining projection is to imagine that the sounds that you are creating are not only filling the room that you are in, but also being projected through the walls, ceiling, and floor, ultimately reaching a much greater distance than your personal practice space. To apply this idea directly, you may want to experiment with practicing your bass outdoors, in a wide-open space. Without walls to reflect your acoustic sound back to you, you'll need to compensate by experimenting with different combinations of techniques until you find a way to reproduce the sound in your head. With this exercise, you can truly work on imagining that the sound waves you are creating are becoming larger and fuller as you work to fill a vast outdoor space.

Apply all of these ideas and techniques to your practice regimen. By making your sound a consistent priority throughout your practice session, you will quickly find the means to best express yourself.

LESSON #16: SPEED DEMON

Playing fast tempos can be a lot of fun. However, it takes time to develop a level of comfort with playing fast so that it *is* fun, rather than simply a challenge. Let's explore some ideas to help increase comfort and confidence when playing "upstairs."

One conventional process to build speed is to practice passages, scales, arpeggios, and melodies at slower tempos and gradually increase the tempo. Use a metronome consistently and transfer this exercise idea to any musical line that you would like to play up-tempo. First, play the line solidly at a comfortable tempo (e.g., 100 bpm). Next, move the metronome to 104 bpm and play the phrase twice. Now move it to 108 bpm and play three times. At 112 bpm, play the line four times, and so on. Once you reach a predetermined metronome marking or you simply can't execute the exercise at whatever the current tempo is, go back to the slowest tempo and do the exercise again.

EXAMPLE 1

Another drill along these same lines is to set a goal of playing a phrase or line 10 times perfectly and in succession. Every time you make a mistake, go back to the beginning, starting again at "one" until you are able to perform the phrase 10 times with rhythmic, dynamic, and melodic accuracy.

EXAMPLE 2

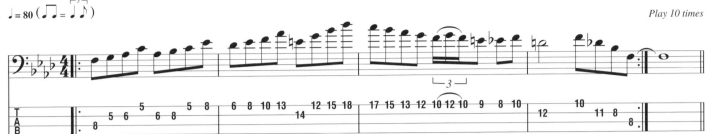

Usually, the majority of your uptempo playing will involve accompanying others with walking bass lines. Although the rhythmic choices are primarily quarter notes, you must have a tremendous amount of stamina and strength to withstand solo chorus after solo chorus. My personal experience has been that the very best way to excel at walking fast tempos is to simply play them in a musical context as much as possible. Try them on gigs, in sessions with others, and with play-alongs. One thing I would suggest when practicing very fast walking is to really try to structure your perception of the time in bigger "chunks." For example, rather than thinking "1–2–3–4" for every quarter note, think in whole measures: 1 (bar 1)–2 (bar 2)–3 (bar 3)–4 (bar 4).

Much of our struggle with playing at high speeds is the ability to think quickly. Dedicated practice for expanding how fast we process and think ahead is invaluable. Additionally, it can be extremely helpful to decide on good-sounding lines and prepare them ahead of time. Use a variety of standard chord changes and write out options that you like and practice them over and over again. Another helpful tip for staying calm while playing "burning" tempos is to rely on some conventional devices to streamline your walking line. Repeated notes or patterns are very useful, as they can anchor the bass line for yourself and for others.

EXAMPLE 3

One more effective trick when working on fast tempos is to attempt to play the line or phrase *faster* than your target speed. After spending some time playing a line at 300 bpm, for example, suddenly playing it at 250 bpm becomes much easier.

LESSON #17: PAINTING IN 10THS

Adding melodic color to our bass lines provides interest for the listener, the other musicians, and us as well. By using the interval of a 10th (a 3rd above the octave) in our lines, we can bring a refreshing alternative to simply outlining the harmony. This first example uses the minor 7th of Am7 and the 3rd of a D7. This technique provides a moment of compelling suspension in the bass line, focusing the listener's ear on the bass and adding interest to the accompanying line.

EXAMPLE 1

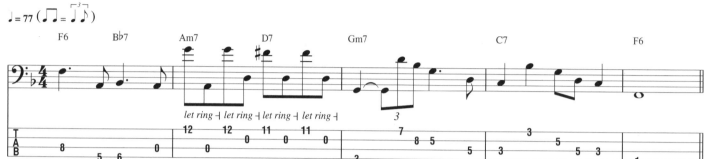

This next line amends the idea slightly, adding the major 9th (the G harmonic) in measure 1. In measures 2–3, rather than the suspension of Example 1, the 10ths here serve to add momentum to the bass line.

EXAMPLE 2

In this example, we aren't using 10ths specifically, but rather playing chord tones in large leaps above the octave. The 5th above the octave is approached chromatically, adding melodic texture to the line.

EXAMPLE 3

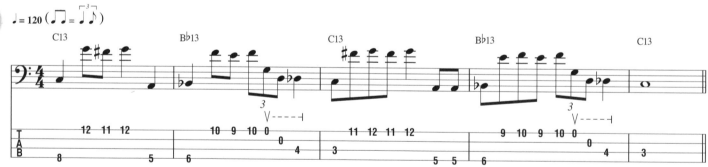

Here is another example of the device from Example 1. The 10ths occur in measure 4 and once again serve to create interest in the melody of the bass line.

EXAMPLE 4

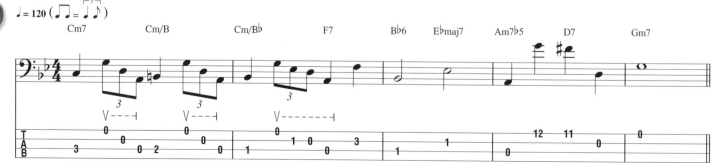

Lastly, here are some exercises that you can practice to further familiarize yourself with playing 10ths and chord tones that exist beyond the octave. Apply this idea to minor chords, varying the rhythms, note order, and direction.

EXAMPLES 5A–B

EXAMPLE 5C

LESSON #18: TWO-FEEL

Often the underdog of bass accompaniment, the two-feel can be a powerful tool with respect to how we arrange our bass lines, create dynamic rhythm, and manipulate musical tension and release. This method was brought to the bass from tuba players, who originally filled the role of the low-end instrument in an ensemble. Early jazz tuba players began to morph a basic brass-band marching beat into a more syncopated and dance-like feel. Bassists (who sometimes were tuba players themselves) continued this primary rhythmic comping of two beats to a bar in a style similar to brass players. The crucial element to remember is that the *rhythmic feel* is top priority.

Listening to great bassists like Arvell Shaw, Ray Brown, Oscar Pettiford, and Israel Crosby teaches us how best to play and use the two-feel concept. In the exercise below, set your metronome at a medium tempo and mentally arrange the metronome sound so that you hear it as beats 2 and 4. Play these simple lines and focus on feeling each swung quarter note, even though you aren't playing it. You want to create as much forward motion and swing with basic half notes as you can.

EXAMPLE 1

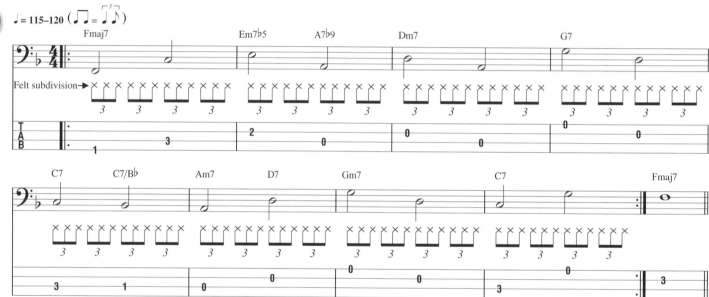

One way to maintain the sense of forward motion in your two-feel line is to place quarter notes in musical and logical parts of phrases.

EXAMPLE 2

Another very effective addition to the two-feel is a well-placed eighth note, which helps to fill out the swing feel. Best described in notation as the last note of an eighth-note triplet, this basic syncopation should move the feel forward to the next note. A common place to play this is on the "and" of beat 4.

EXAMPLE 3

Here is an example of a much more active two-feel. Notice, however, that all the extra notes ultimately serve to create a sense of movement, dance, and swing.

EXAMPLE 4

LESSON #19: THE JAZZ WALTZ

Playing in 3/4 time as a jazz waltz requires more than simply eliminating a quarter note from 4/4 meter. The jazz waltz feel has a distinct rhythmic quality that should maintain the buoyancy of swing while alluding to the common sensation of perceiving the time in "one." The underlying triplet motion should remain constant throughout, even though half notes and dotted quarter notes are often played.

Work through this first example, a sparse bass line, to acquaint yourself with playing broadly through the chord changes while feeling a strong "one" at the beginning of each bar. This is especially effective when playing a fast waltz.

EXAMPLE 1

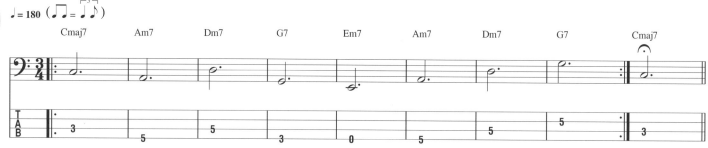

Similar to ornamenting a two-feel, you can add quarter notes and eighth notes to your lines, which help to define the time and keep the line moving in a musical way.

EXAMPLE 2

Another common way to perceive and play in a jazz waltz is to emphasize dotted quarter notes. A dotted quarter note splits up a bar of 3/4 evenly, which allows us to hint at multiple meters while still technically playing a waltz.

EXAMPLE 3

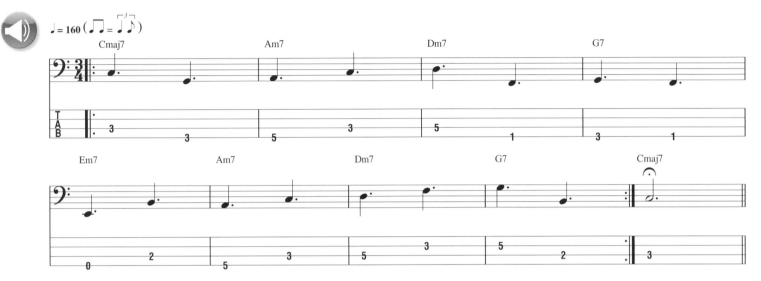

Here is an example of an active waltz feel that uses the aforementioned devices.

EXAMPLE 4

We should always be thinking about how we arrange our own accompaniment while playing a song. It's important for everyone on the bandstand to take responsibility not only for the time and playing well with each other, but also for working to shape each song with dynamics, tension and release, and interest for the listener. I've found it effective to use, in succession, the types of subdivisions featured in this lesson to slowly build tension, and then release it with walking quarter notes when the timing is right, musically.

LESSON #20: ODD METERS

Over time, jazz musicians have grown to incorporate more odd-meter playing into their compositions and performances. For example, 5/4 and 7/4 have become relatively standard time signatures, used in a variety of settings. While some musicians regularly explore and utilize more dense or complex meters, we'll focus on these two in this lesson.

Playing in 5/4 meter is something many of us are familiar with due to the immense popularity of Dave Brubeck's composition "Take Five." The recorded bass line in this classic song clearly defines the most common rhythmic pattern used with this meter.

EXAMPLE 1

Using this pattern, we can apply similar rhythms to a variety of chord changes. It can help to imagine a measure of 5/4 as being broken into a section of 3/4 and a section of 2/4.

EXAMPLES 2A–C

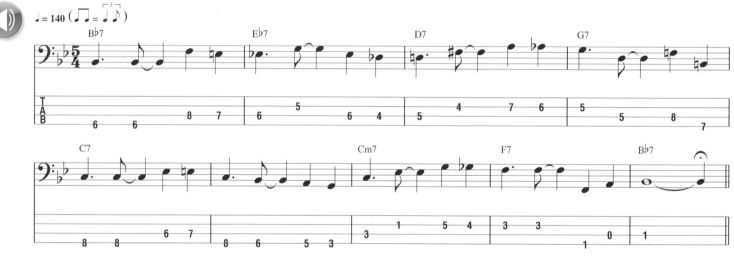

A similar angular quality to the rhythm is found in 7/4 meter. There is also a basic clave used to "ground" the feeling of this time signature. Here is the basic pattern and examples of using it over chord changes. Like 5/4 meter, we can break 7/4 into two sections; in this case, one section of 4/4 and one section of 3/4. Using 7/4 and 5/4 as stepping stones in your exploration of odd meters will give you a solid foundation for future performances.

EXAMPLES 3A–C

LESSON #21: DOUBLE-STOP BLUES STANK

Here's a tool to add interest to your lines and solos. By using the internal tritone of a dominant chord and scooping into these simultaneously played notes, you can evoke a real "moaning" or bluesy quality from your line. The tension created by the major 3rd and minor 7th of the tritone provides a good, mildly dissonant "crunch," while the slide into this interval gives a vocal aspect to the phrase.

This technique tends to be more effective when played relatively high on the neck and approached from a somewhat lower note or phrase. Here are a few examples of where you might play these double stops. You'll notice that you can use these same two notes for two different dominant chords, depending on which note you consider the 3rd and which you consider the ♭7th.

EXAMPLE 1

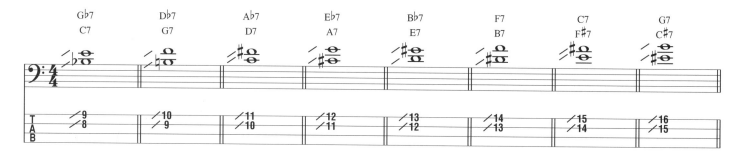

Next, spend some time getting comfortable with shifting from lower notes to the higher register.

EXAMPLE 2

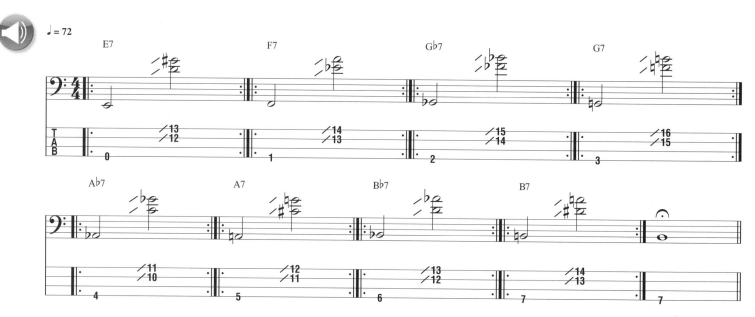

Now let's put these double stops into action by creating a repetitive bass line over a 12-bar blues form.

EXAMPLE 3

You can also use this technique within a solo to add color and an element of surprise.

EXAMPLES 4A–B

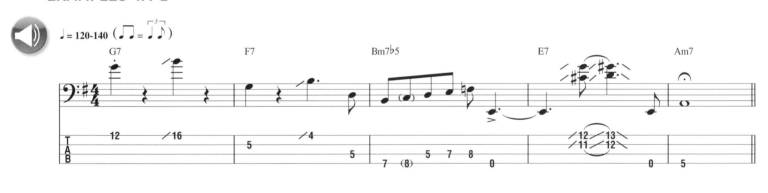

If you spend some time researching your own ways to incorporate double stops into your playing, you can quickly add them to your repertoire of expressive techniques.

LESSON #22: SPINNING THE WHEELS

This simple concept, which the legendary jazz bassist Ray Brown called "Spinning the Wheels," is less a technique and more a study in arranging your bass line with tension and release. The idea is to play a single, repeated note in an appropriate musical place and quickly transition to a walking line after some tension has been created. The simple movement from a static bass line to a dynamic one can provide harmonic and rhythmic tension, interest and variation at key points in a song, and ground the ear to the key center and time feel. You can think of the effect as a bow being pulled back to release an arrow or perhaps gunning an engine before throwing a car into gear. The subsequent release of tension (a shot arrow or a shift into overdrive) is a very compelling musical experience.

Here are some examples of how this device can be used. Note that they begin four bars before we actually begin "spinning the wheels" so you can get some sense of the musical context. I find this method most useful when applied to the beginning of a new chorus for a soloist that you are accompanying. As you work with the soloist and ensemble, use it to structure the overall peaks and valleys to give life to the music. You can apply it to the very beginning of a new solo or at mid-solo in order to push the music to a new level.

In these first two bass lines, the concept is subtle. Play the root on the downbeat and repeat it for the whole bar. What adds a little extra weight to the execution here is that the note is carried over to the downbeat of the next measure, slightly extending the feeling of suspension and tension.

EXAMPLE 1

EXAMPLE 2

These next examples demonstrate how we can add extra tension by playing the 5th of the chord as the repeated note. This will imply an unresolved dominant (V7) chord in relation to the written chord, and when the built-up momentum is released, it's an even more powerful tool.

EXAMPLE 3

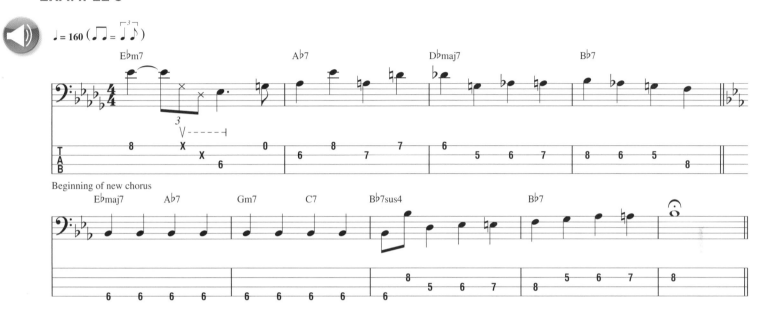

EXAMPLE 4

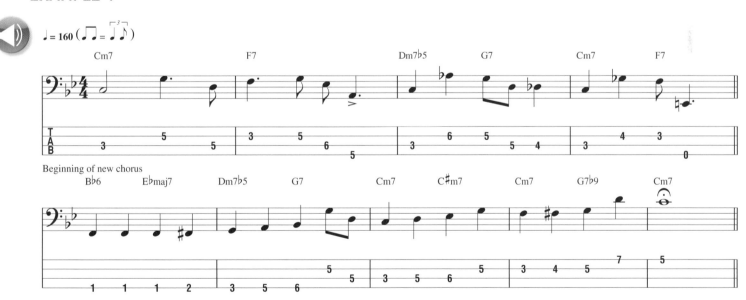

It's really best to hear this concept in context, so when you come across this device in your own listening or playing, notice the effect on the band and the music. Experiment and have fun!

LESSON #23: CLEF DIVING

An interesting effect to use in your walking lines is a device I call "clef diving." This is a tension-and-release strategy that works well to both provide variety to your bass line and to quickly switch fingerboard positions as you play. The idea is to walk into the higher register, usually over at least a couple of measures, and then suddenly drop to a lower part of the bass. This can serve to maintain the momentum of a line, as you may quickly run out of room in the thumb position. Rather than working your way back down in step-wise motion, the surprise of this large interval jump has a nice musical effect. Notice in this first example how the upward motion begun in measure 5 continues over three full measures, with the multi-octave jump occurring on the "and" of beat 1 of measure 8.

EXAMPLE 1

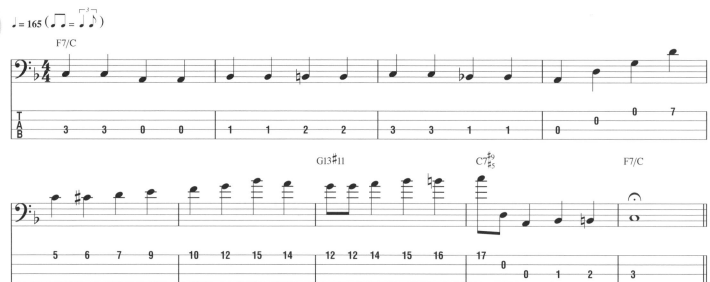

Here is a slightly more subtle example of a clef dive. Note that measure 9 would be the beginning of a new chorus (and perhaps the entrance of a new soloist). The preparation for the dive would also be occurring alongside the other musical tools that the rest of the ensemble is contributing as the band raises the energy level for a new chorus.

EXAMPLE 2

Because the highest notes in a line occur on the G string, the open D string typically will be a strong choice to play as you jump down. In addition to being the next/closest string, playing an open string will provide you with a little extra time to shift your hand from the higher positions back to the lower part of the neck.

EXAMPLES 3A–B

So far, we have seen examples of the open D string being played as an eighth note on the way back down the neck. Here, the clef-diving effect is still utilized, but without the aid of the interim note. Also, the previous examples have generally jumped down to a note on the A string. However, we can also use the open D string or, for a really wide interval, the open E string when appropriate.

EXAMPLE 4

LESSON #24: THE E-BOMB

To "drop a bomb" in the musical sense, a player will create his or her own dramatic statement during a song. Often used when referencing a drummer's performance, this device can strongly punctuate a phrase, be the peak of a solo, or spur the ensemble to reach for more intensity. Both the preparation and the execution of this forcefully emphasized moment are important, and a frenzy of tension-building will often climax with this effect.

Although more understated than the drums, bass bomb-dropping has the potential to be just as effective. Besides the setup of the moment, it's very important to play this concept with conviction. Part of the appeal of this tool is the strong and unquestioned attitude in its execution.

While almost any note can be used in this effect, our low E string contains a great deal of innate potential for volume and power, and I've found it a great choice for dropping bombs. In these examples, notice that the bombs are played after a quick, eighth-note preparation and syncopated on the upbeat, adding even more heft to the feeling. Pay attention to the articulation here: the downbeat is slightly staccato and the upbeat bomb is very strongly accented.

EXAMPLES 1A–C

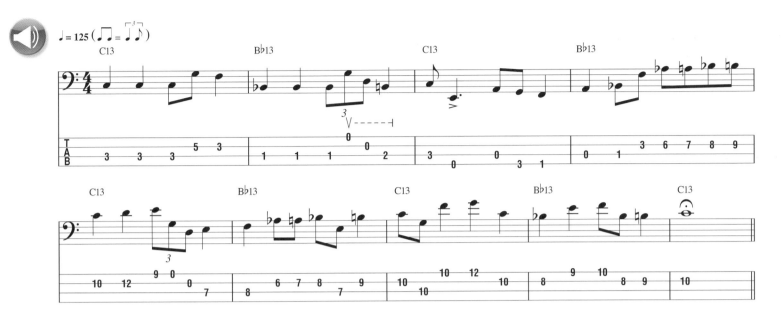

Here are some other ways to use the E-string bomb. While not exactly the same recipe as the previous lines, these examples can still be a commanding musical statement.

EXAMPLES 2A–B

If you are able to apply this device in your own playing, you should find it a rewarding tool for adding color to your bass lines.

LESSON #25: DROP IT LIKE IT'S HOT

Creating tension and release in our bass lines and solos is an important factor in making the music engaging and expressive. By combining triplet drops, string raking, and a slow build up to a high register and its quick release to low notes, we can make a big impact on the intensity of our walking. These first examples conspicuously use the devices mentioned above. A sense of anticipation and tightening is created after an ascending line goes into thumb position. This buildup of energy is quickly released with a multi-octave triplet drop via string raking to allow us to reach the lower notes.

EXAMPLES 1A-B

Here is a similar example, but notice how effective this combination of ideas is when it climaxes at the beginning of a new chorus.

EXAMPLE 2

This version of the idea is implemented in concert with the drums. As the drummer plays a fill in measures 3–4, he or she creates the same kind of tension that we might build from an ascending line. The bass completes the idea with a triplet drop to a walking line, fulfilling the release.

EXAMPLE 3

In this bass line, the sense of anticipation is created not by an ascending line, but rather by a couple of measures of walking in the upper register.

EXAMPLE 4

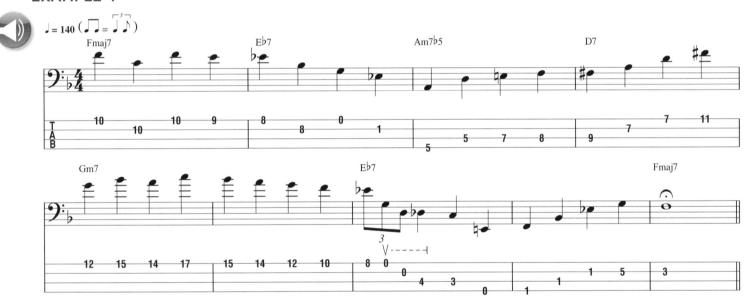

This last example features a variation on the idea. Although not quite as dramatic as the bass lines above, the effect demonstrates how the basic concept is useful in multiple ways.

EXAMPLE 5

LESSON #26: SLIPPERY TIME

One of the great things about improvised music is the ability to go anywhere within a song. Jazz allows us immense freedom to express our individuality and creativity, and "slipping" between time feels can be a great tool for building excitement and variety. Let's explore some ways that we might move to new places, rhythmically, by superimposing or alluding to modulations of meter, rhythm, and beat placement. First, let's visit the concept of polyrhythm, whereby two or more conflicting rhythms occur simultaneously. You're most likely familiar with many kinds of polyrhythm, as it is an almost fundamental aspect of music as we know it. Here are some examples that may be recognizable to you.

EXAMPLE 1

A hemiola is a three-against-two feel. Here, two dotted quarter notes occupy the same space as three quarter notes.

EXAMPLE 2

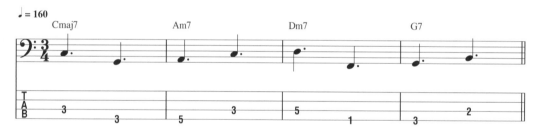

Another commonly used polyrhythm involves playing dotted quarter notes in 4/4 time.

EXAMPLE 3

The term metric modulation refers to a shift in note groupings or the perception of tempo in a song. For our improvisational purposes, let's use this phrase to identify the concept of manipulating the perception of time feel in a song. Using the previous examples as guides, we can begin to explore cross-rhythms to use in our playing. Using the dotted quarter-note figure from Example 3, we can impose the feeling of a slower quarter note over the established tempo.

EXAMPLE 4

And by thinking of the dotted quarter notes in a hemiola as 12/8 meter, we can create a similar effect.

EXAMPLE 5

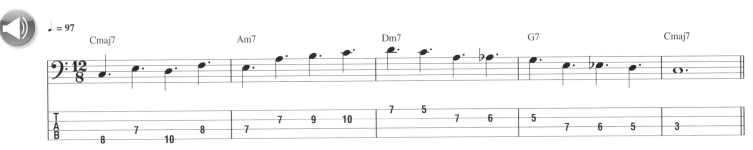

By grouping triplets together as if they were quarter notes, we can create the illusion of speeding up the tempo, completely changing the time feel.

EXAMPLE 6

This next example adds another rhythmic layer while shifting time. Here, dotted quarter notes are superimposed over the 4/4 feel created by the hemiola's dotted quarter notes. We are definitely slipping away from a jazz waltz!

EXAMPLE 7

LESSON #27: OSTINATOS

Our role as an accompanist for others should include more than just walking four beats to a bar. It's the responsibility of each member on the bandstand to tastefully contribute what they can to a soloist's moment in the spotlight, as well as to the broader music itself. An ostinato—a repeated note, figure, or pattern within a song—is one such way that we can contribute ideas while comping. Let's examine some ideas for incorporating ostinatos into our bass lines.

A simple application of this idea would be to play a portion of a walking bass line over and over again for effect. The feeling of suspension or hesitation from this effect creates a dynamic change when shifting back to conventional walking.

EXAMPLE 1

A useful manifestation of this concept is to create a small, repetitive melody during the walking bass line that involves more than just quarter notes. When utilized appropriately, this can be a great way to participate in the musical conversation while maintaining the primary role as accompanist.

EXAMPLES 2A-B

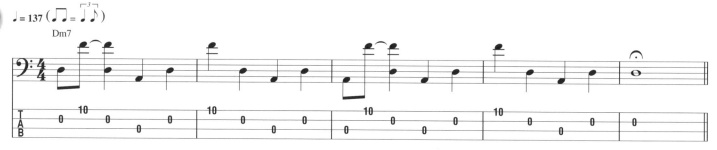

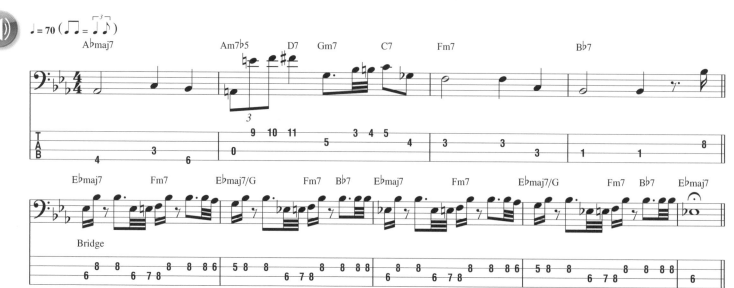

Technically, an ostinato is defined as an exact repetition of a phrase, but the term can also be used more freely. For example, when riffs are transposed to fit different chord changes, the entire bass line can be referred to as an ostinato.

EXAMPLE 3

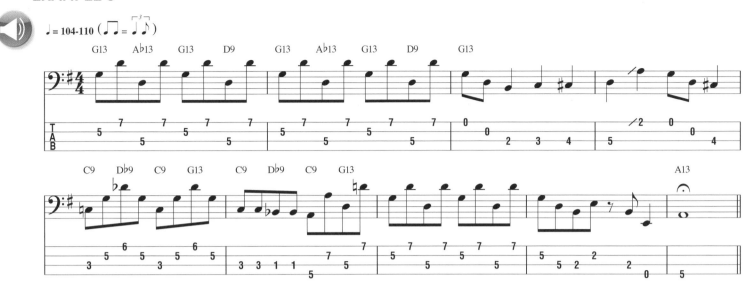

The ostinato can also be a rhythmic pattern whose notes change along with the progression.

EXAMPLES 4A-B

You may also choose to insert an ostinato in your line to create dissonance and suspense. By playing a repetitive figure that clashes with the stated harmony, a sense of musical strain is created.

EXAMPLE 5

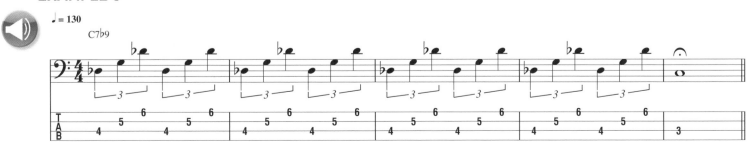

LESSON #28: PEDAL POINTS

Context is important when making great music. The way in which we set one musical thought against another plays a big part in the creative process, and using pedal points is a prime example of how to present a unique idea that opposes another in the context of the song. The premise of pedal points is to sustain one note or tonality in the bass while the harmony above it moves from chord to chord. Often begun in consonance, the pedal usually creates dissonance as the harmony changes.

EXAMPLE 1

A pedal point can be as basic as suspending the dominant chord of the key over diatonic harmony.

EXAMPLE 2

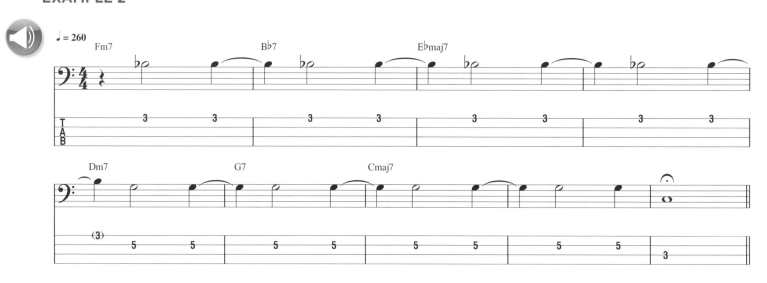

It can also simply be a sustained note that serves as an anchor between chords in motion.

EXAMPLES 3A–B

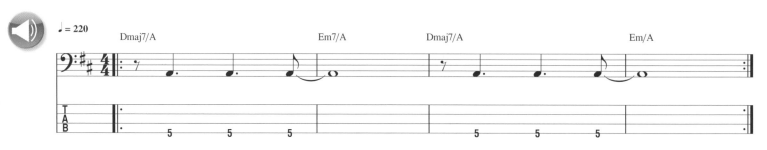

A pedal point can be more than just one note, too, and is often played as an ostinato figure.

EXAMPLES 4A–C

These bass lines would not have the same impact in a different context, and it's important to note that your musical decisions should be in response to the moment. Use a piano to investigate different sounds on your own, playing a pedal note or figure in the left hand and different chords in your right. I'm sure that you'll discover some amazing sounds.

LESSON #29: UPPER-REGISTER TENSION AND RELEASE

In this lesson, we'll focus on building and suspending tension by remaining in the higher register. Walking lines tend to travel across the fingerboard naturally and musically. By deliberately choosing to stay in the higher register, we can create a feeling of anticipation. Because we are setting parameters on the lines that we are creating, there is a subtle sense of arrangement and thoughtfulness.

This first bass line is an example of walking exclusively in the higher register.

EXAMPLE 1

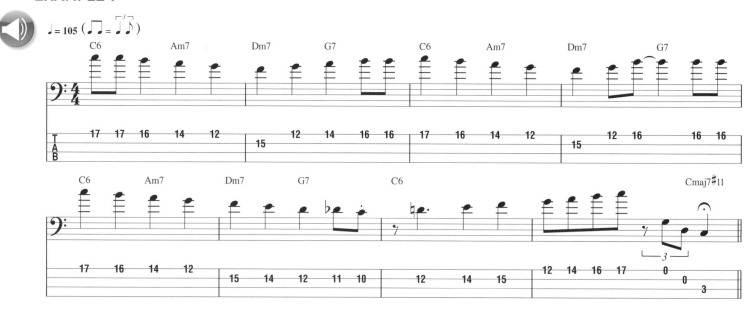

Next, let's look at how we might connect the higher and lower registers as we travel down the fingerboard.

EXAMPLES 2A-B

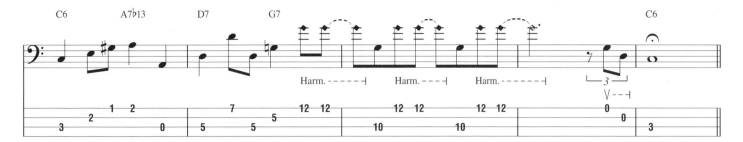

To demonstrate how we can utilize a quick release from the upper register, here's a bass line in thumb position over rhythm changes.

EXAMPLE 3

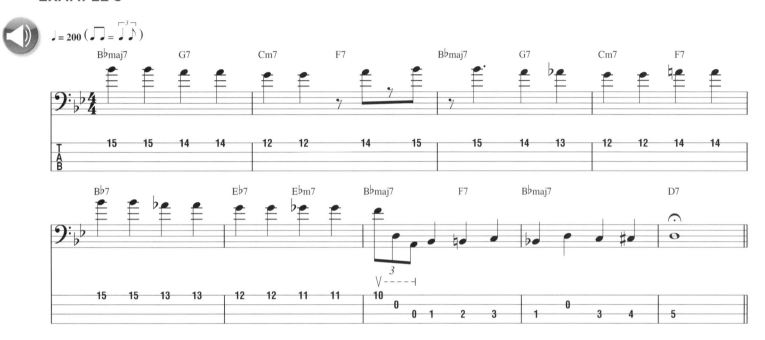

Of course, we can combine other tension and release ideas, like ostinatos and "spinning the wheels," with this method of walking.

EXAMPLES 4A–B

This kind of study is also helpful for keeping us familiar and comfortable with notes in the higher part of the instrument, where many of us feel a bit less confident. By studying and creating your own bass lines in these positions, you'll surely feel stronger about playing in them.

LESSON #30: REHARMONIZING CHANGES

One of the great things about the conventional role of the bass in jazz music is that the walking bass line is a powerful force in defining the harmony of the song. We have the ability to control a huge range of harmonic possibilities, all by playing one note at a time. With a single decision, we can turn a tune inside out, and may redirect the entire performance as a result.

The act of manipulating the harmony with our bass notes is something that we usually do naturally, though it is often understated. For example, every time we play the 5th of a chord, we are implying—albeit subtly—the dominant chord on that beat. Here are some examples that demonstrate how we might choose to reharmonize the chord changes in a very deliberate way.

The first substitution revolves around the very common ii–V–I cadence in jazz. Because the notes that make up the ii chord in a given key are shared by the V chord, we can always imply the ii chord where a dominant chord exists. This will add a bit more color to the harmony and slightly delay the sound of the dominant chord.

EXAMPLES 1A–B

Chromaticism is a staple of walking bass lines. When we are thinking of the harmony that we may be adding to a tune, chromatic lines take on additional weight.

EXAMPLES 2A–B

Diatonic substitutions or additions are a great way to add motion to the harmonic progression. Therefore, it's very important for us to understand the function and inner-workings of jazz harmony as we apply this useful concept.

EXAMPLE 3

Tritone substitutions are also commonly alluded to in our bass lines. Because the "tritone sub" contains the same tritone interval of the dominant chord that it is replacing, and the root of the substitution usually creates chromatic movement in the bass line, it's an extremely strong and effective sound to use.

EXAMPLES 4A–B

Lastly, when we examine how different bass notes affect the harmony that exists on top of the root, there is a nearly limitless variety of options. The master bassist Ron Carter has developed this skill so profoundly that his reharmonizations can be songs in and of themselves. By understanding harmonic function, movement, and theory, we can bring dynamic additions to our performances by using only our bass line note choices.

EXAMPLE 5

LESSON #31: MORE WALKING DEVICES

Creating bass lines really accesses the fundamentals of jazz improvisation: we need to understand the harmony and the form, play the instrument well, and react appropriately to the musical moment, all while creating melodies that are supportive and functional. And, as with all improvisation, we need to be open to various tools and possibilities that serve these functions.

This lesson features a few concepts that can be applicable to various musical scenarios and should prove helpful in our improvisations in general. For example, just as we can add a iim7 chord to its relative V7 chord, we can also *remove* the iim7 when it serves the moment, such as when the soloist is creating something that calls for it or because doing so enables us to create a better bass line in that instance.

EXAMPLE 1

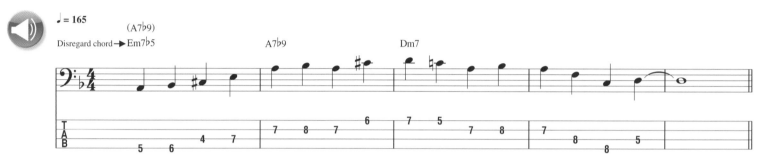

Another choice that we can make is to change the harmonic rhythm by delaying a resolution.

EXAMPLE 2

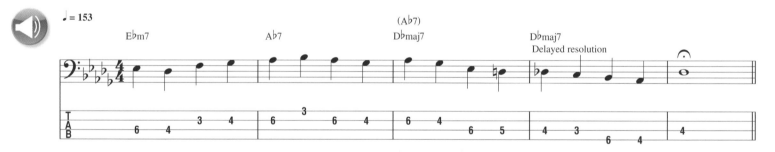

We can also anticipate an upcoming resolution or chord change.

EXAMPLE 3

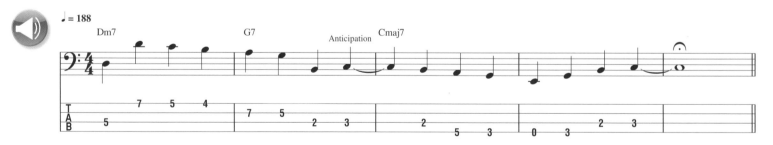

And we can add color to quarter notes by sliding between them.

EXAMPLE 4

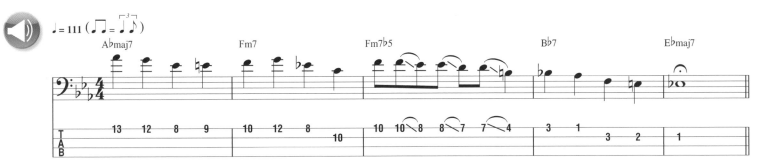

We can also add variety to quarter-note lines by deliberately articulating certain notes in interesting ways.

EXAMPLE 5

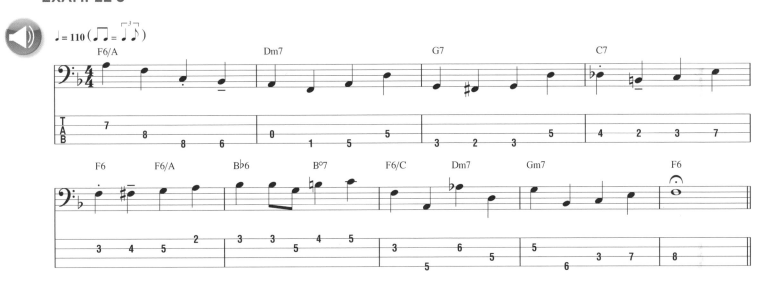

Another option is to make our note choices via voice leading. In this way, the continuity of the line at that moment becomes more important than specifically outlining the changes.

EXAMPLE 6

LESSON #32: WALKING CHALLENGES

There are a number of reoccurring harmonic progressions that we encounter in music. One example is chords that resolve around the cycle of 4ths. Progressions like those found in rhythm changes, blues forms, and many of the standards from the American songbook follow generally recognizable and commonly used harmonic movement. Because of this, we tend to have experience in creating walking bass lines for these progressions.

But what about a more dense or unfamiliar chord pattern? Musicians have always experimented and manipulated the harmony of songs and are constantly creating new arrangements of standards. Additionally, the contemporary harmonic language has grown increasingly sophisticated, so we may often encounter unfamiliar chord progressions as we play or write original material. Let's look at a few of the more unconventional progressions and examine how we might improvise a bass line over them.

A longtime benchmark for musicians has been the ability to play over "Coltrane changes." The process of figuring out how to improvise over these harmonic structures teaches us so much, as you can choose to do everything from simply playing roots to creating a long bass line of chromatic movement. This can be best achieved by really taking time to think about the available notes from chord to chord. Go slowly and focus on connecting the changes.

EXAMPLE 1

The music of Thelonious Monk often contains chromatic harmony that can require some thought to negotiate. For example, when creating walking lines, you can choose to expand the written harmonic rhythm or disregard one of the chords altogether.

EXAMPLE 2

Personally, I've found standards like the first four bars of the A-section of "Like Someone in Love" to be tricky for me to play without some forethought. Because you have the multiple messages of the clearly delineated bass movement against different harmony on top, some discipline and practice is required to create a musically cogent line.

EXAMPLE 3

Other examples of wonderful yet complex chord progressions are found in the compositions of Wayne Shorter. They can be troublesome to understand from an analytical standpoint, but are logical and musical in their own special way. While the progressions may be unconventional, my advice for playing them can be applied to *all* music: familiarize yourself with the song. Play, sing, study, listen, and practice the music as *music*, rather than a series of exercises. Once you familiarize yourself with the song, your bass lines will be profoundly informed by it.

EXAMPLE 4

LESSON #33: MELODIC WALKING LINES

It was a revelation to me when a teacher of mine shared that walking bass lines are independent melodies. For whatever reason, this wasn't a perspective that I had considered, but from that point on, my goals for creating lines changed. It also provided me with new paths to explore, as having the priority of improvising good melodies, in addition to providing a functional foundation, provided exciting challenges that I had not yet sought out. In this lesson, we'll explore some examples of bass lines that use this melody-as-a-priority concept.

In this first example, notice that only three of the eight bars contain the conventional method of playing the root on the downbeat, yet we can clearly hear the harmony outlined throughout. The melody stated in measure 1 is extrapolated throughout the changes, with a sense of call and response and melodic momentum. By using notes closely related to the diatonic harmony, the line maintains a consonant yet interesting sound.

EXAMPLE 1

Here is a bass line that's played over a form with less harmonic movement—the blues. With more time to improvise over a single chord, longer melodies can be created. Notice that there is more chromatic movement here, as both the form and the harmony of the blues allows for the utilization of approach notes and passing tones.

EXAMPLE 2

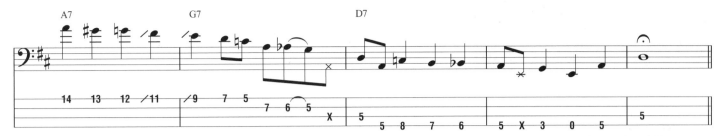

Here is another example that is primarily diatonic. There are four distinct melodies here, each two bars long, that follow one another logically and musically.

EXAMPLE 3

It's important to note that the method that I refer to in this lesson is about creating a melody within the conventions of a standard walking bass line. There are certainly countless ways to accompany in an ensemble that differ from this often-used and familiar style of playing. My point here is to think differently about the typical walking bass accompaniment. To demonstrate this, play through the melodic walking line in Example 4A and notice that, with some minor adjustments, the bass line becomes a nice solo phrase (Example 4B).

EXAMPLES 4A-B

HUMP LINES

In the context of swing, "hump" refers to the quality of the rhythmic feeling and the attitude of the time. It has to do with momentum, a relaxed intensity, a sense of dance, and relentless forward motion. Even though this can't be conveyed in written notation, there are some devices that we can use in our bass lines to engage and perpetuate the hump in our playing and, hopefully, in the entire band.

Many years ago, a peer of mine, a fantastic bass player, told me that certain bass lines and note choices can make the band swing more. He didn't explain much, if at all, and I was left with a bit of a mystery to be solved. Over the years, I've tried to think about this while listening, studying, and playing. Here are a few samples of some of what I believe are answers to that mystery.

A clever device for surprise that can really start off a solo section with excitement is a slightly delayed entrance. This is absolutely more effective if the whole rhythm section applies it simultaneously. Simply waiting a beat or half a beat to enter after a dramatic buildup is really powerful.

EXAMPLES 1A–B

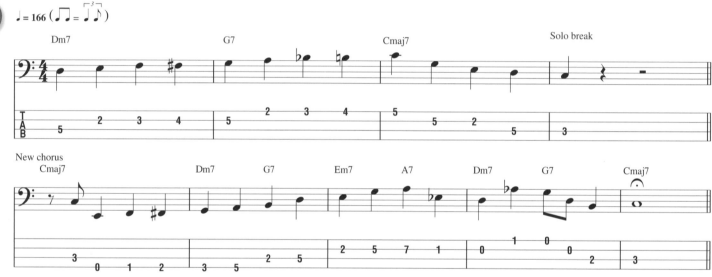

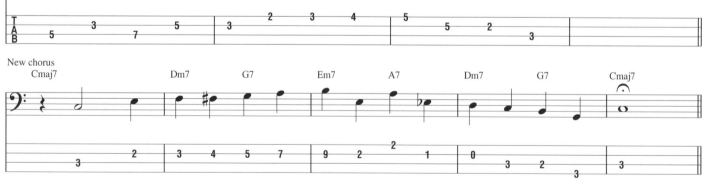

Similar to the previous example, a quick setup and release of a fundamentally strong line will set the tone for a swinging performance.

EXAMPLE 2

Devices like skips and triplet drops will greatly add to the sense of achieving a "hump" in the sound of the band. Simply playing them well yourself will enforce and encourage the rest of the ensemble to swing together.

EXAMPLE 3

Another idea is a buildup of tension and release by walking into the high register and suddenly dropping down to the lower part of the bass. An additional benefit of this technique is how it spurs the time feel forward, helping to provide the rhythmic attack that we are looking for.

EXAMPLE 4

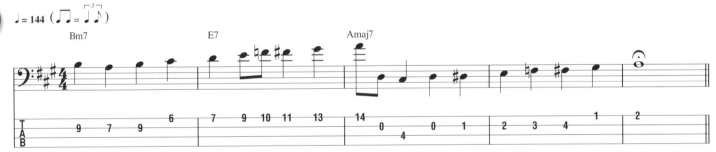

In order to swing, a common notion among bass players is to play beats 2 and 4 in our walking lines physically harder. While this does allude to the feeling of swing, the reality is much more subtle. Often, I hear students approaching their walking this way and it invariably feels heavy and plodding. The emphasis does exist, but it's understated. A different way to emphasize beats 2 and 4 is by repeating a single bar that places chord tones on those beats, which are further strengthened by the chromatic approaches on beats 1 and 3.

EXAMPLE 5

LESSON #35: SECRETS TO A GREAT BASS LINE

Unfortunately, there are no real shortcuts to greatness. Part of what creates mastery is the work needed to succeed, and without the disciplined effort involved, we may find it impossible to achieve. That said, it's important to clearly define our goals as we strive to be virtuosos in our craft. The following list covers some of the elements that I believe make up a great bass line in the tradition of Paul Chambers, Arvell Shaw, Ray Brown, Oscar Pettiford, Charles Mingus, and Wilbur Ware, among many other exceptional bass players of yesterday and today.

Many of the characteristics of a good bass line are directly in line with what we may view as qualities of great music in general. When we apply them directly to our bass line accompaniment, they can become specific signposts for assessing the music that we are creating. Clearly, our most important goal should be to make good music, regardless of our instrument. In the broadest sense of the idea, "good music" can mean anything, as it's entirely subjective. But, if we are striving to master performance in or be informed about a particular style, there are some objective benchmarks that we'll want to pursue. Personally, I feel strongly that, as musicians, it's our duty to seek out knowledge, to be curious, and to be persistent in our attempts to assimilate the vast amounts of information about music. Though this is generally a life-long pursuit, many find these infinite mysteries to be solved irresistible.

Let's take a look at the list and then I'll elaborate on a few of the items. A good bass line should have:

▶ Good sound

▶ Accurate intonation

▶ Good feeling for listeners and the ensemble

▶ Rhythmic accuracy and control

▶ Swing with forward motion and buoyancy

▶ Support for the ensemble and soloist

▶ Harmonic awareness, accuracy, and controlled alternatives

▶ Relentlessness, confidence, and strength

▶ Cogent melodies

▶ Appropriate dynamics

▶ Musical variation in rhythm, melody, and harmony

▶ Awareness of and responsiveness to the form

▶ Connections, even abstract, to the song's root melody and harmony

We can group some of these into larger headings, too. For example, *technical* aspects of creating a good line involve facility on the instrument, getting a good sound and accurate intonation, rhythmic accuracy, and dynamic control. By working on fundamentals of playing the bass, we are able to better express ourselves in the music as a whole. If we are struggling to play in tune, for example, we are both distracted from the moment and less able to articulate our musical vision. We'll have a much harder time reacting to what's happening on stage and connecting with the music, the audience, and the other musicians. We have to do our best to understand and master the techniques involved in playing the bass so that when we are actually *creating*, we are as unencumbered as possible. This idea also applies to why we study traditional methods of technique. Over time, bassists have continually refined the physical aspect of playing so that we can be free to improvise without constraint. Hand- and body-position norms exist to aid in our stamina and strength, not simply as rules to be blindly followed.

Some *performance basics* are listed here, too. Connecting to the song's melody, harmony, and form mean that we are *playing the song*—a simple but often overlooked aspect in jazz performance. Often, we get caught up in our attempts to play something that we've practiced, find something that's harmonically hip, or impress an audience. This can easily pull us away from participating in the moment or considering our relationship to the tune. Additionally, we need to at least understand and be aware of—if not "respect"—the form of the song. How we express our awareness of the form is up to each of us individually. But no matter how loose or rigid it might be, it's our responsibility to know and play the form.

Also, bassists rarely play solo, and never in a vacuum. Not only are we required to perform at our best as individuals, but we usually exist as part of some kind of ensemble. Ideally, each musician on stage has an equally valid presence there, and we should strive to accept what musical offerings exist. And as bass players, we are so often in a supportive role, that listening intently to our musical colleagues is paramount.

Swing feeling is a phrase that encompasses several of the previous ideas too. To "swing" or "be swinging" is about the rhythmic feeling, but it also can describe much more. When we swing with others, there is a feeling of camaraderie, respect, and a sense of welcoming joy. We should strive to speak and listen, to hear and be heard, and to honor the musicians and musical moment. To be rhythmically swinging with others, we need to be relentlessly pursuing a sense of forward motion that maintains a relaxed intensity. Our notes should have a bounce that's matched with a grounded consistency and, at the very least, allude to the dance aspects of this unique rhythmic attribute.

We want to manifest confidence, support, and strength in the swing that we are creating and, in turn, help to make others feel good, too. And "feeling good" is a summation of the overall goal. It's not that we are seeking to falsify some saccharine ideal of sweetness or happiness, but rather to participate in creating a musical space where everyone can experience a satisfaction in the journey. We should hope to foster such a sense of openness, emotional vibrancy, and passion that the concerts we play ultimately enrich the lives of listeners and musicians alike.

Aspects of *musical basics* are also in this list. Variation in rhythm, melody and harmony, logically improvised melodies, and dynamic control are a few foundations of good music. Our bass lines should naturally reflect these basics. Having a depth of musical vocabulary enables us to access various tools for expression, and the deeper the vocabulary, the more profound our expression can be. So it's incumbent upon us to examine, assimilate, and manipulate a wide range of rhythmic, melodic, and harmonic language. By studying the lineage of the master musicians who came before us, we can understand and utilize concepts of musical logic and dynamism. Sam Jones, Ron Carter, Israel Crosby, Jimmie Blanton, Walter Page, Milt Hinton, Scott LaFaro, Jimmy Garrison, Slam Stewart, and Red Mitchell are just some of the names to add to those listed previously for us to study.

Our goal is not to simply follow patterns that we've learned, but to function as conduits for our internal voice as we simultaneously create musical moments with those around us. Walking bass lines are so much more than consecutive quarter notes and downbeats occupied by the root of a chord; at their best, they are the marriage of individual and group improvisations that can transform a space or take a listener on an emotional journey.

LESSON #36: OPEN HOUSE

Using open strings in our bass lines and solos provides several benefits: there is less effort involved in creating a large interval (e.g., between an open string and a higher note), the open strings can be a quick source for checking our tuning, we can save small but important bits of time when moving between positions, and they are convenient alternatives for passages that require tricky fingerings.

Referencing the large intervals that we can create, let's take a look at two examples of walking bass lines that use open strings for a variety in sound and an angular melodic feeling.

EXAMPLE 1A

EXAMPLE 1B

Now let's use open strings to create large intervals in some solo phrases.

EXAMPLE 2A

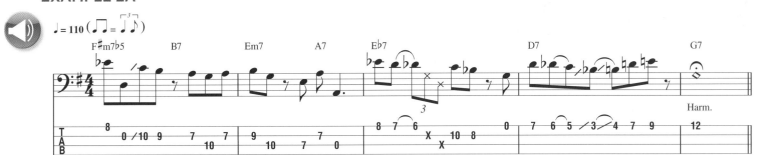

EXAMPLE 2B

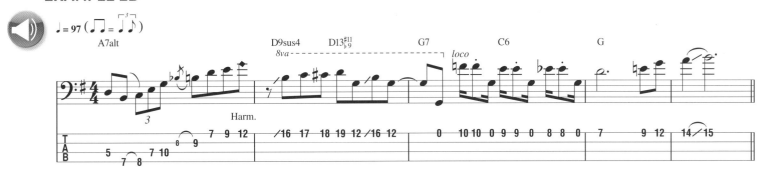

Here are two examples that mostly use open strings as ornaments, rather than as arpeggiated harmony, as in Examples 1A–B.

EXAMPLE 3A

EXAMPLE 3B

I encourage you to incorporate open strings into your own playing—and have fun!

LESSON #37: BASS LINE SHAPES

When we look at a wide stretch of a walking bass line, it will generally fall into one of four categories: linear, angular, landscape, or two-tiered. It's important to think of our lines in bigger portions than just the bar of the moment so that we can assess the quality and direction of the accompaniment. It's also helpful to study the visual notation of the bass lines of great players, as it gives us clues as to how they approached the music from a macroscopic level. Additionally, it's an interesting exercise to place the shape of the bass line in the context of the music that is surrounding it. You may find that angular lines match a soloist's fervor, or perhaps a smooth landscape might be a counterpoint to that same solo intensity.

Linear lines are phrases that strongly favor continuous progress in one direction. Multiple measures featuring a bass line that continually moves up in register is an example of a linear line. So, too, are walking notes that continue down the fingerboard for an extended period.

Here is an example of an ascending linear line:

EXAMPLE 1

And here is a descending linear example:

EXAMPLE 2

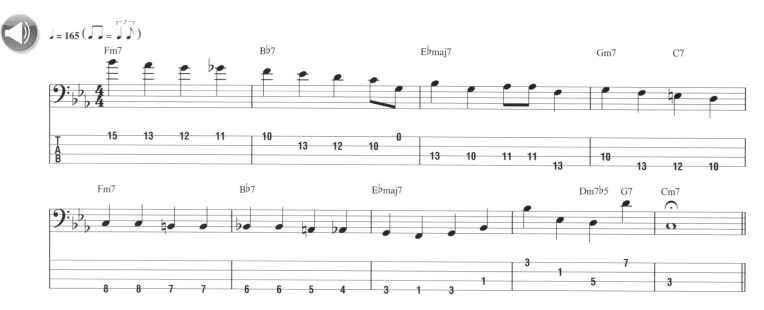

Bass lines that would be considered angular can have either multiple measures of intervals that vary in direction or a whole phrase that "jumps around" more than a linear bass line.

EXAMPLE 3

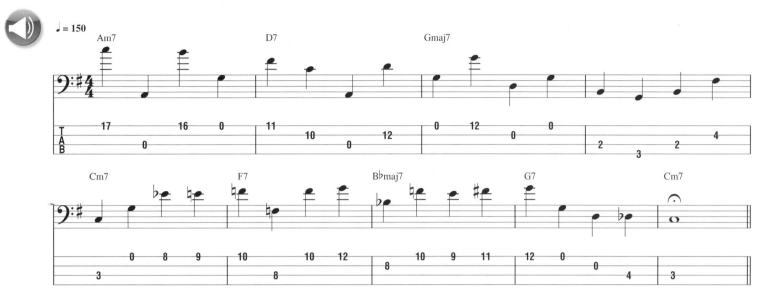

Landscape lines form a continuous but varied up-and-down motion, as if the notes graphically represent hills in the distance.

EXAMPLE 4

Two-tiered lines could also be considered "call and response" bass lines. They are also angular, but create the illusion of two separate lines occurring side by side.

EXAMPLE 5

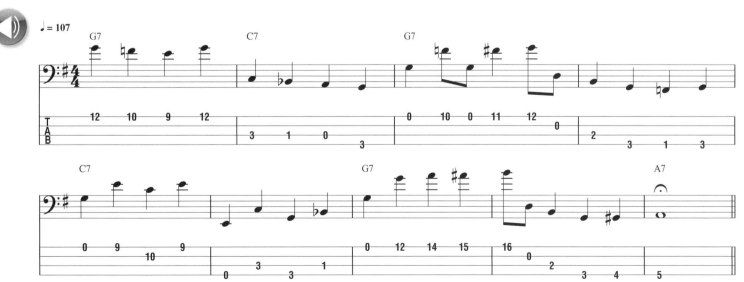

Take some time to explore your own bass lines, as well as those of other great musicians, and I'm sure that you'll find a wealth of interesting ideas for walking-line shapes.

LESSON #38: TRIADS

The triad can be a powerful tool. By superimposing an upper-structure triad over a chord, you can achieve a very complex sound, and using triads and their inversions in our walking bass lines provides many opportunities for interesting note connections. Here are some drills to delve deeper into triads on your instrument.

Our first example features an F major triad with many rhythmic variations. The idea is to explore the fingering, sound, and feel of the triad to become more familiar with it. This kind of exercise should be applied to the major, minor, diminished, and augmented triads in *all* keys. You should also create your own rhythmic variations.

EXAMPLE 1

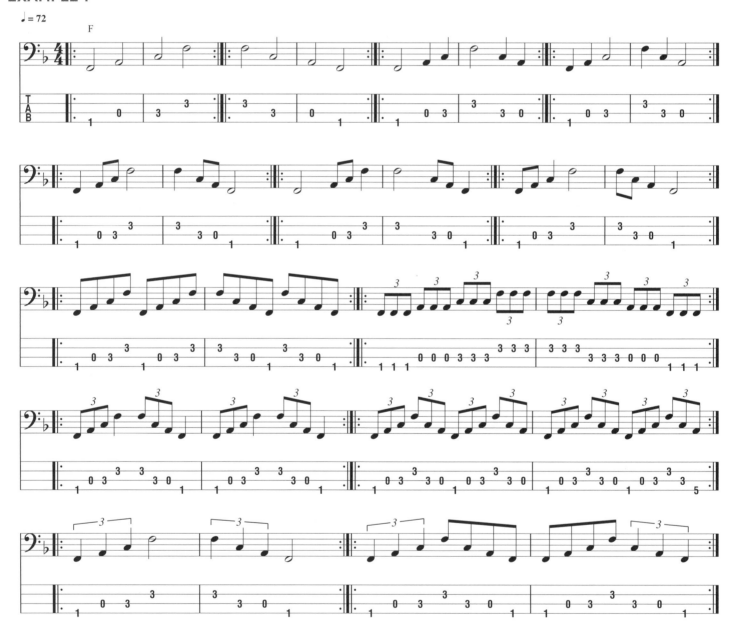

Example 2 features different types of triads and their two inversions. You'll want to cover each and every one across all keys and triad qualities.

EXAMPLE 2

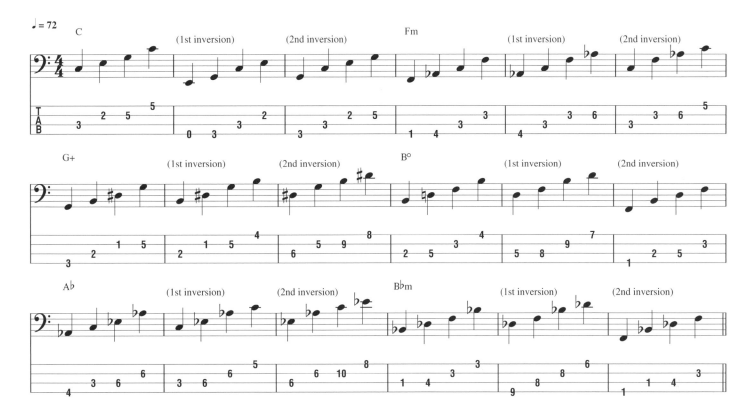

Next is a short example of how you might use triad inversions in a conventional walking line.

EXAMPLE 3

Lastly, have a look at this simple but effective exercise. By mastering all of the triads and inversions with increasing tempos and across the fingerboard, you'll have vast amounts of material to extract and use in solos. When applied appropriately, portions of these triplet figures always sounds good as a phrase in a solo.

EXAMPLE 4

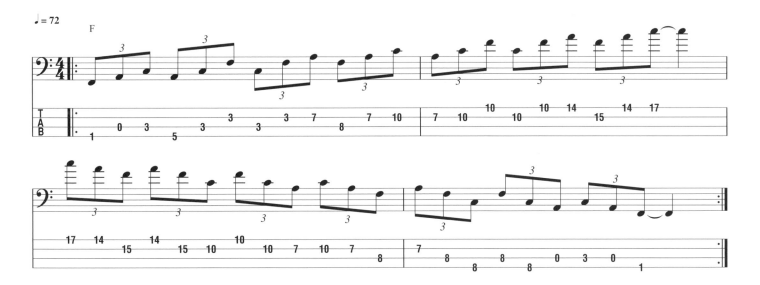

LESSON #39: INVERTED SEVENTH CHORDS

As with triads and their inversions, deeply familiarizing ourselves with seventh chords and their inversions is an invaluable benefit. We reinforce our understanding of harmony, strengthen our connection to our instrument, and learn the whole fingerboard. It is important to work on every chord type, from every possible root note, so that we can be as flexible as possible in our playing.

First, let's quickly review the standard chord qualities that are available.

EXAMPLE 1

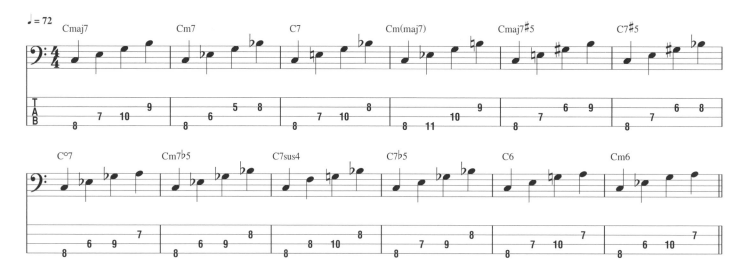

Next, let's outline each inversion. With seventh chords, there are three inversions, rather than two.

EXAMPLE 2

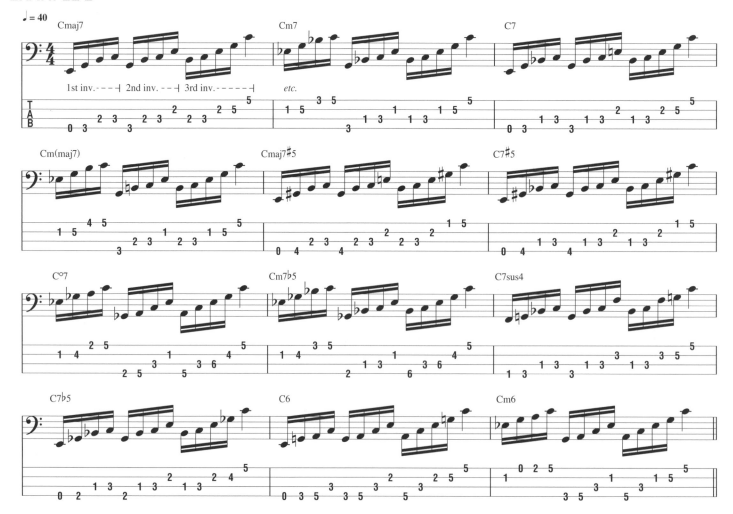

It's very helpful to arpeggiate the chords of a song so that you can become comfortable with different kinds of root movements and get deeper into the skeleton of the tune itself.

EXAMPLE 3

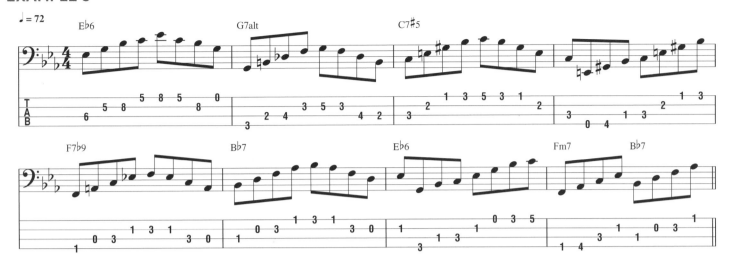

Now we'll take the chord progression from Example 3 and use various inversions to create a walking bass line with just arpeggios.

EXAMPLE 4

And here are the same chords, but with other scale tones and passing notes to demonstrate how inversions can help us smoothly connect the changes. This exact idea applies to solo phrases as well.

EXAMPLE 5

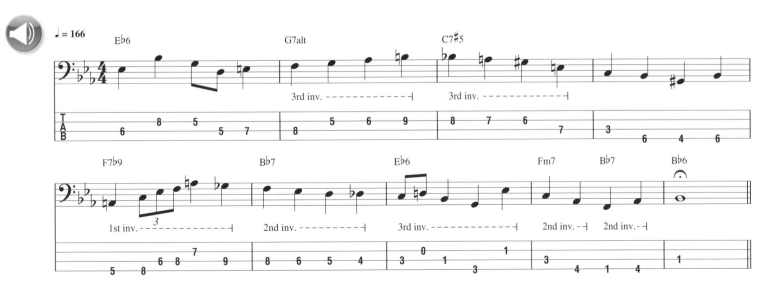

LESSON #40: SCALES IN INTERVALS

There are many ways to become more familiar with scales on our instruments. One effective way is to play them in intervals. With this approach, we encounter jumps that are less common, which in turn, gives us a workout on the fingerboard. Additionally, we are constantly reinforcing these useful interval sounds in our ear, making it easier to hear, identify, and utilize them in performances and transcriptions.

This first example is created by using a strictly diatonic major scale and repeating it in intervals. You'll notice that the quality of the intervals change, depending on where you are within the scale. For example, 3rds, 6ths, and 7ths can be either major or minor. With 4ths and 5ths, there is one interval that becomes augmented and diminished, respectively.

EXAMPLE 1

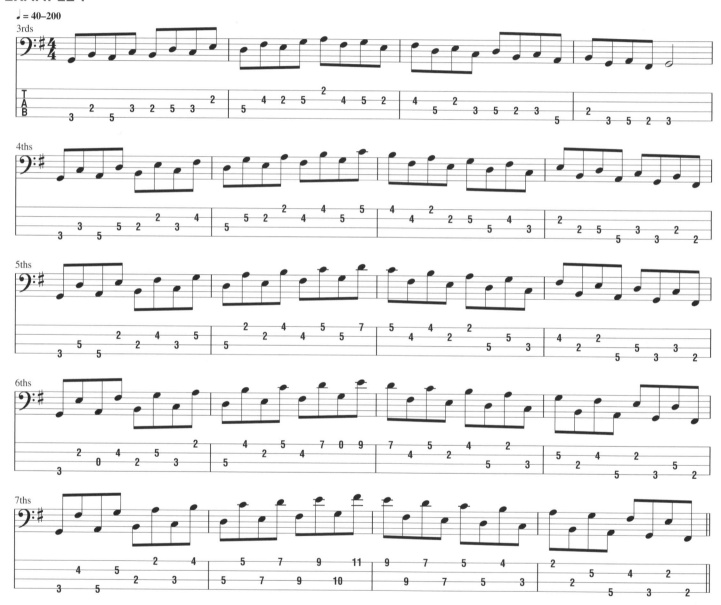

Here is the same process, but with the harmonic minor scale. Pay attention to the fact that, because of the different scale, the qualities of the intervals change, too. Play this same exercise will all major and minor scales and their relative modes.

EXAMPLE 2

Play around with all of these intervals by starting and ending a sequence from different parts of the scale, varying rhythm, tempo, and register. So far, these examples have begun on the root and stayed within the range of about an octave. What would an exercise look like if we used all the notes from the scale that are available across the range of a conventional four-string bass? Take a look…

EXAMPLE 3

♩ = 40–200
C major scale in 4ths, from lowest available note to highest

There are several more ways to explore scales, so keep searching for new ones to strengthen your comfort level with these basic building blocks of improvisation.

LESSON #41: PURE INTERVAL CYCLES

As the basic building blocks of melody, intervals are critically important for us to master. This series of exercises is geared toward "stacking" intervals one after another. Rather than holding to a key center or scale, the idea is to play each cycle as sequential intervals. The exceptions are the chromatic, symmetrical diminished, and whole-tone scales, which follow a pattern of repetitive minor 2nds, minor 3rds, and major 2nds, respectively. First, choose one base note as your starting point. For our purposes, let's choose an A. Now begin to build sequences of intervals, starting with a minor 2nd. The result is simply a chromatic scale.

EXAMPLE 1

Next, move to major 2nds.

EXAMPLE 2

Now let's begin to group them together in broader sections. Here are minor and major 3rds:

EXAMPLE 3

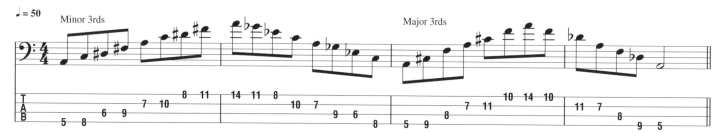

Perfect 4ths, tritones, and perfect 5ths are next. You'll quickly notice that you are limited by the range of the bass, so you'll have to jump down several octaves to continue the cycle.

EXAMPLE 4

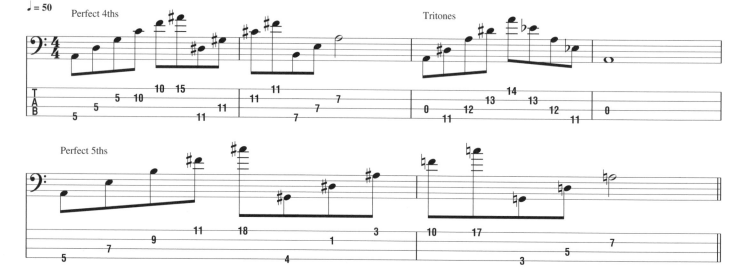

Minor and major 6ths come next in our drill.

EXAMPLE 5

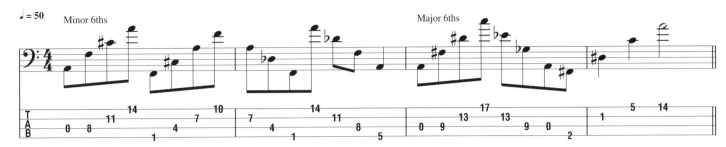

And finally, minor and major 7ths complete the overall pattern.

EXAMPLE 6

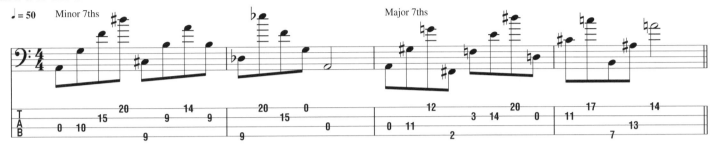

Now let's put all of these intervals together into one giant exercise. Be sure to work from all 12 available starting notes.

EXAMPLE 7

LESSON #42: COLLAPSING SCALES

When we improvise, we want to be able to access a full range of available notes for the sound of the moment. Because we may find ourselves in unplanned or unexpected places on the neck during the creative process, we need to be adept in our fingerboard knowledge. I call these "collapsing scales" because the drills get progressively smaller.

The idea is to first choose a scale—for example, C Lydian with a ♭7th (Lydian dominant)—and then apply the following procedures. Your first pass will be the full range of the instrument, from high to low and low to high. So, this will be a scale from the lowest available note on the instrument that is in the scale to the highest (let's choose a high E on the G string).

EXAMPLE 1

Your next starting note will be the next available note in the scale, ending on the note just *before* your previous ending note. For C Lydian dominant, you now start on the F♯ in half-position and end on the high D on the G string—the note in the scale just before your previously played highest note, E.

EXAMPLE 2

Continue this process through the degrees of the chosen scale, with your starting note chosen from the next, ascending scale tone, and your ending note chosen from the next, descending scale tone. Notice that I've marked the lowest and highest notes of each "pass" with a circle and encompassed each pass with a bracket. You can easily see here how the sections become shorter and shorter.

EXAMPLE 3

Now reverse the pattern!

LESSON #43: MOBILITY SCALES

Much of successful improvisation has to do with how quickly our mind works in the moment. As we play, we have to be constantly evaluating and making decisions based on the *now*. This isn't some magical skill that suddenly comes to us, but rather is developed through patient and consistent practice and preparation. Here's a simple but powerful tool for connecting chord changes and training ourselves to make quick adjustments as we improvise.

As the lesson title indicates, our hands and mind need to be agile and mobile during our performances. This can be aided by the exercise below, where we set up specific parameters for fast switches in real time. The general idea is to play continuous chord scales that elegantly and swiftly change as the harmony of the song changes. The first step is to choose which chord scales we will use. Let's look at the progression in Example 1. Play through these changes slowly until you develop a confident grasp of the scales in succession.

EXAMPLE 1

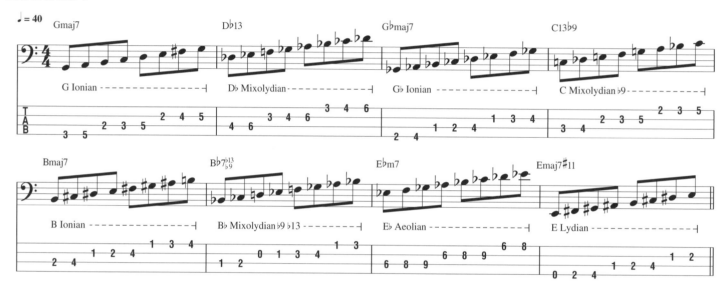

Next is the crux of the exercise: playing a walking bass line through the chord changes with your chosen chord scales, adjusting the scales as the harmony changes. Wherever you are on the fingerboard, choose the next closest note from the new chord scale. You aren't starting from the root of each new change, but rather continuing in the direction of the line that you are playing. That said, start the drill on the root of the first chord change, at the lowest register of that note on the bass.

EXAMPLE 2

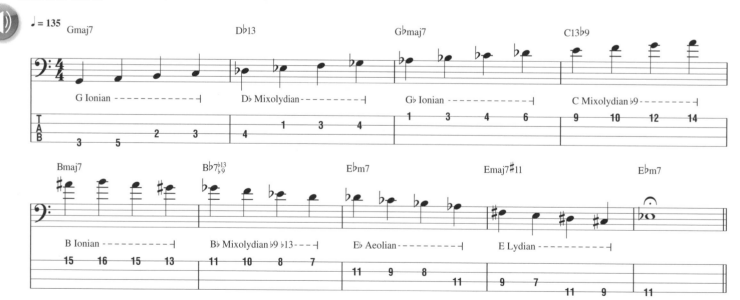

Now start the exercise on the lowest *note* on the bass that fits into the first chord scale. Continue to change scales as the harmony changes, playing ascending and descending lines as the register dictates.

EXAMPLE 3

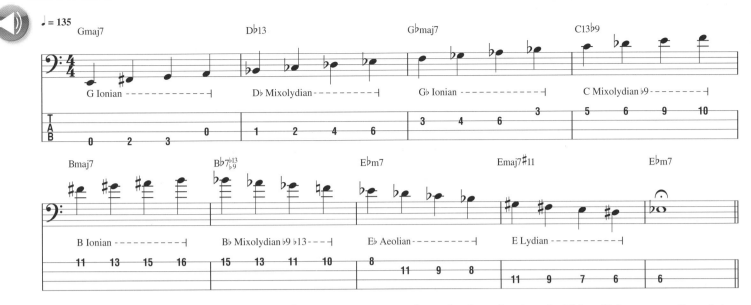

To get deeper into the exercise, choose different starting notes from the first chord scale. This will force your lines into different places, which will cover more of the options that invariably occur in improvisations.

EXAMPLE 4

Next, increase the density of the lines to eighth notes, eighth-note triplets, or 16ths notes. This will ensure that you're able to apply the same mobility to faster passages or solo lines.

EXAMPLE 5

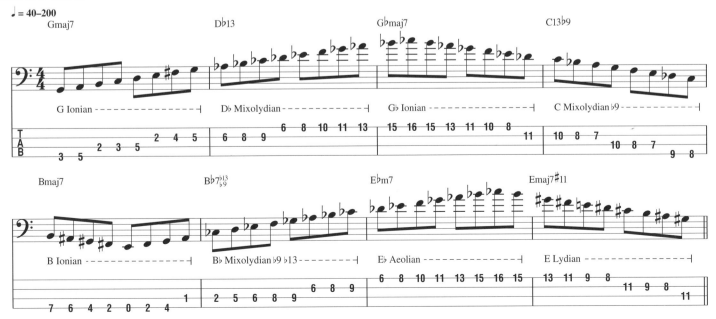

LESSON #44: SOLOING DEVICES

Satisfying musical statements tend to contain a few basic elements, such as variation or tension and release. Let's explore a few conceptual tools that we can use to add satisfying moments to our solos.

The first device is the often-cited "play/rest" approach. Simply put, by honing your ability to wisely edit your phrases, you'll have a much greater impact on the listener. One rudimentary exercise to work on this idea is to choose predetermined segments of time when you'll play or not play. For example, here is an example of playing for two bars and resting for two. With the play/rest approach, you can choose any parameters you'd like, and variation in your practice approach is key.

EXAMPLE 1

Another soloing device is to experiment with ways to incorporate the melody of the song into the solo. This can be a fantastic idea to help start a solo, as the material is already there and sounds good. Once you've alluded to the melody, you can continue to build upon your ideas from there.

EXAMPLE 2

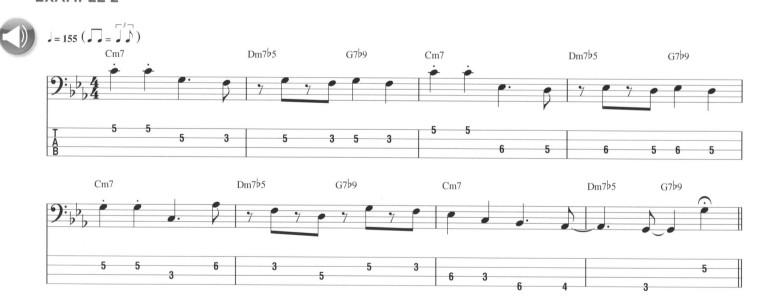

Call and response is a familiar tool that always works well when executed correctly. By "trading" ideas within the solo, you allow the listener to latch onto your solo in a new way.

EXAMPLE 3

The amount of rhythmic activity or density in your solos can be a great source for variety. Carefully crafted musical statements will ebb and flow, creating a sense of organic expression.

EXAMPLE 4

These are just a few of the many things to consider when creating your own improvised solos. I encourage you to listen to master musicians as your final source of information for soloing devices. By choosing what sounds good to you, and figuring out *why* it sounds good, you'll be well on your way to making great music yourself.

MOTIVIC DEVELOPMENT

A motif is a single musical idea that occurs in a generally small unit in time. Motifs are usually followed by a short period of rest to distinguish them as individual statements. By creating a motif and applying various types of logical adjustments to it, our solos take on understandable and interesting progressions that are enjoyable to listen to.

After creating the original motif, the first change that we'll make is to amend the note choices, keeping the rhythm the same.

EXAMPLE 1

Another option is to extend the motif. First, play the original idea, rest, and then play the original idea again but with an extended melody.

EXAMPLE 2

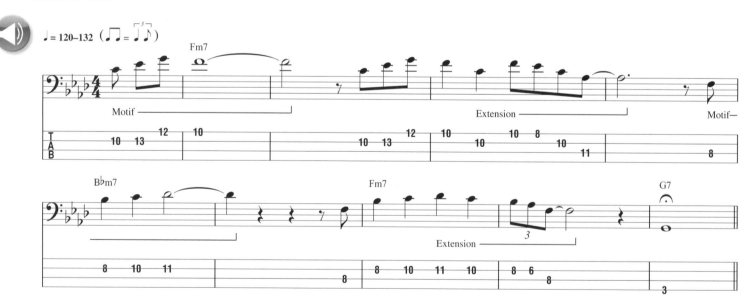

If we play a slightly longer or multi-motive phrase, we can build on the idea by resting and then repeating a section of the original phrase. That is, we'll play a *portion* of the original idea, instead of repeating the whole motif.

EXAMPLE 3

By combining the aforementioned ideas, we can state an original theme, rest, repeat a portion of it, and then immediately add material to the fragmented section.

EXAMPLE 4

Another idea is to add elements of rhythmic variation to the repetition of the motif or fragment. Maintain the same notes or note shape, but condense or expand the rhythmic pattern.

EXAMPLE 5

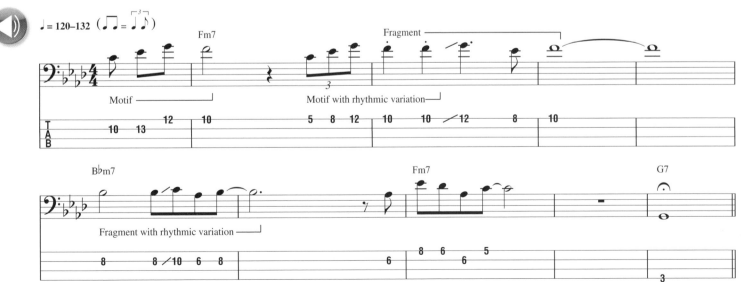

This lesson is just a meager sample of the exercises available for motivic development. Seek out more!

LESSON #46: UPPER-STRUCTURE TRIADS

Triads that result from combining other notes of a chord scale, and contain an available tension from that scale, are sometimes called "upper-structure triads." Essentially, you are building triads from within the chord scale of the root chord quality. For example, for a C major seventh chord, where we are using the Ionian mode as the chord scale, a G major triad (G–B–D) can be created from the 5th (G), the major 7th (B), and the major 9th (D).

EXAMPLE 1

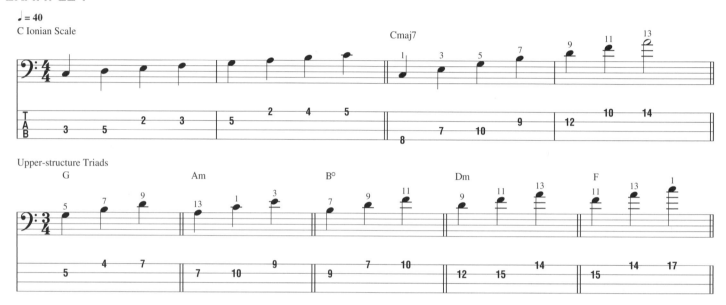

In general, as you choose these triads, avoid those that contain a tension that would clash with the root chord. With our example of a C major seventh, we would avoid the B°, Dm, and F major triads, as they all contain the note F, which clashes with the Cmaj7 sound.

Let's begin to think about applying this to improvisation. First off, we'll need to choose the chord scales for each chord in the progression that we are working on. Here are some options:

EXAMPLE 2

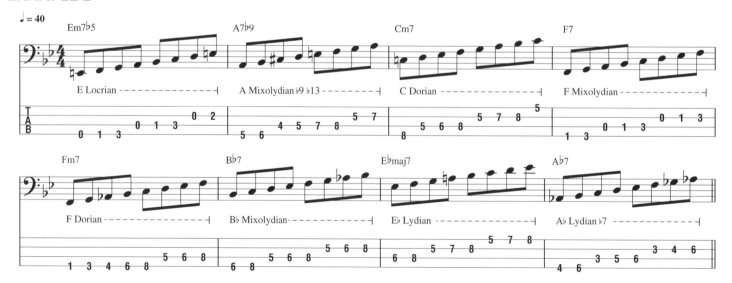

Now that we have chosen our chord scales, let's decide on which upper-structure triads we will use. Write these triads above the original chord. Often, the major triad options will sound good because they have a clarity that sticks out, but other options are equally valid. Experiment with different options to find sounds that *you* like.

EXAMPLE 3

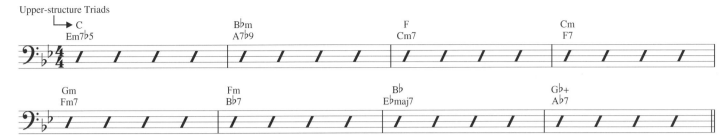

Take a small rhythmic motif and repeat it for each bar, changing triads as the harmony changes.

EXAMPLE 4

Now create a more organic solo, but still restrict your note choices to the predetermined upper-structure triads. Work on making smooth connections between the changes, even within the limits of these triads.

EXAMPLE 5

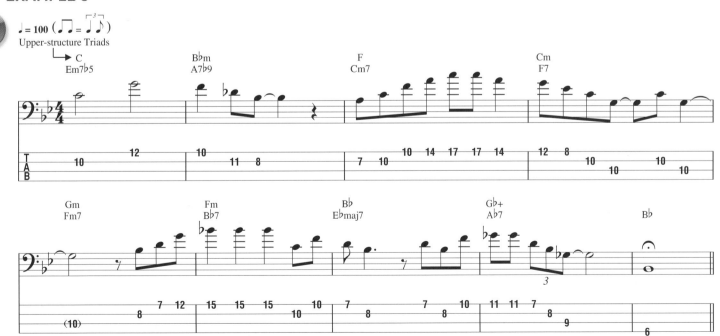

Once you're comfortable with limiting yourself to the upper structures, apply the concept to your normal soloing. You'll find interesting ideas for melodies with this technique. There are many options to delve into, and I hope that you enjoy your journey of finding new sounds to make your own.

LESSON #47: SCALE AND ARPEGGIO PRACTICE TREE

The study of music is a lifelong one, and practicing scales and arpeggios is an ongoing process for most of us. Because anything is possible in the idealized version of improvisation, we're called upon to have a grasp of huge amounts of information. While trying to organize all of the possibilities with respect to practicing the triads, scales, and arpeggios that we encounter, I developed the "tree."

What concepts we work on and how we work on them are nearly limitless, although using this tree gives us a specific number: 9.93×10^{21}. That is, 9.93 times one *sextillion* (a word that I discovered while writing this lesson!). It's certainly impossible to cover all of these options in a single lifetime, but I think that the information here is valuable for finding viable alternatives to our normal practice routine. You can choose to experiment with just one category—for example, articulation—or decide that you want to incorporate many of the different choices into each day. You can mix and match at will and find a wealth of motivation.

First, you'll choose which scale, arpeggio, or triad to practice and the context in which you'll place them. Once these are chosen, begin to decide on the variables that you'll use as you work. For example, if we're going to practice a ii–V–I chord progression in B♭ major (Cm7–F7♭9–B♭maj7), we'll spend time on the chord scales: C Dorian, F Mixolydian ♭9, and B♭ Lydian.

Now that we have chosen our scales, let's play them in ascending and descending eighth-note triplets, slurring the first two notes of each triplet. Additionally, let's choose a medium tempo and 3/4 time. We'll stay in the low-to-middle register of the bass and start each scale from the fourth degree. We will also use two fingers on our plucking hand and all available fingers on our fretting hand, starting with the index finger.

EXAMPLE 1

Another option may be to practice a D major triad over a Gm(maj7) chord. Let's play the triad in second inversion, from the lowest available note on the bass, and ending in thumb position. We'll alternate soft and loud dynamics as we play eighth notes in 5/4 time. The tempo will be slow and we'll use one finger on our plucking hand and three fingers on our fret hand. We will play all the notes as legato as possible.

EXAMPLE 2

With just these two examples, you can quickly begin to see how many variations are possible when we practice. Choose a method that works best for your personality. I'm a pretty linear thinker, so I like to approach things in order, but you may prefer to pick and choose randomly. While the space here doesn't allow for every single option available, I hope that this practice tree will inspire you.

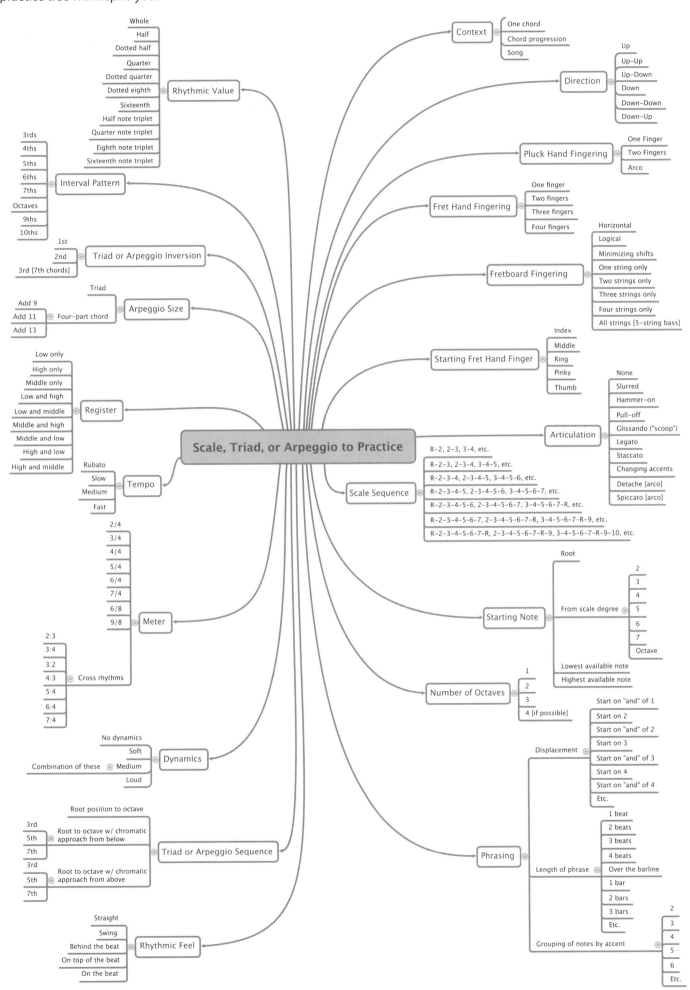

LESSON #48: BOUNCE AND SWING

In swing music, having a sense of "bounce" in your time feel can add a lot of life to the music. Bounce is the sensation of lilt and motion that a good swing groove inspires; it's the keystone for performing music that others want to dance to, and when shared with the ensemble, makes a musician's experience that much more fun.

Let's take a more in-depth look at how our note sounds are connected to articulation and instrument setup. In general, a sense of bounce results from some separation between consecutive notes. We're speaking here of the amount of sustain and decay of a given note. More experienced musicians can create bounce without a formal separation between notes, but, for practice purposes, let's stay with this idea.

There are three parts to the sound of a note: attack, sustain, and decay. In order, these terms refer to the initial moment that the note is plucked, the length of time that the note stays at the attack volume, and the period of time during which the note's volume fades away. Notes with bounce tend to have a strong attack, relatively short sustain, and quick decay.

To be clear, we're not talking about playing notes as harsh staccatos, beating the bass relentlessly in a series of blister-causing bebop lines. There is great subtly involved in creating bounce, and the best way to learn this feeling is to simply listen over and over again to great musicians who have this sound in their playing. Play along with recordings of them and do everything that you can to emulate their feeling.

That said, by examining bounce from a clinical perspective, we begin to turn our minds towards adopting that sound. Studying the idea brings you closer to it in every way and feeds your subconscious learning processes. So, even if your first attempts at manipulating bounce sound forced, you'll make progress by doing the work and consistently trying to hear the sound and feel in your head.

Here are two contrasting audio examples of a simple C major scale. They're played at the same tempo, but notice how the second example has more of a light feeling of movement.

EXAMPLE 1

By adding slight articulations and note-length variations to the phrase, we're able to create a whole new sensation in the music.

It may be surprising to hear, but your instrument setup can clearly affect the attack, sustain, and decay of your notes. Stereotypically speaking, when bass strings are raised higher from the fingerboard, they will have a shorter sustain and faster decay. And string choice can make a huge difference as well. For example, gut strings have an extremely short sustain and fast decay, while typical metal strings tend to resonate for a longer period of time.

String height affects the bounce feel, as a preset short decay that's caused by higher strings will naturally create the necessary space between notes. This touches on one of the difficulties of playing swing music with the electric bass, where the instrument is usually optimized for long and sustained notes. Without allowing the natural breath between notes, walking and solo lines can seem "mushy" or "soggy." I encourage electric players to think about how they can manipulate their note lengths in service of creating the bounce feeling. It may be different strings, higher action, damping strings, or most likely, a combination of all of these.

Study this example of a solo in the style of Ray Brown, where certain articulations are clearly marked and should point you to some places to focus on.

EXAMPLE 2

Listening to amazing musicians like Dizzy Gillespie, Sonny Rollins, Wynton Kelly, Woody Shaw, and Clifford Brown will surely provide you with many chances to hear bounce in their music. Bassists like Sam Jones, Israel Crosby, and George Duvivier all had a strong sense of bounce in their sounds, as did the often-cited Paul Chambers, Oscar Pettiford, and Ray Brown.

Listen to the masters and imitate everything that you hear, from the note choices to the swing feeling, and you'll be well on your way to creating something that's uniquely your own.

Pocket, groove, hump, swing, and tip—all of these words are associated with the rhythmic attitude in straight-ahead jazz. This elusive, sometimes controversial, and nearly-impossible-to-notate feeling is part of what I believe makes jazz so great. It's a gift to the world that our elders created in America and, in my opinion, should be cultivated and cherished. Because this music is oral and aural, it is critical that, in order to absorb and replicate the swing feeling, we listen to great players. There are no books, technical devices, or apps that will teach us; the recordings and live performances are the source, period.

All that said, it is helpful to be able to use the written word and musical notation to try and further communicate ideas. In that spirit, let's look a bit more closely at the most often used notation device to try and encapsulate swung eighth notes.

As you've probably seen and heard before, swing can be summarized with a polymetric or cross-rhythmic notation. An undercurrent of triplets is felt within the quarter notes and eighth notes. The first two parts of the triplet are tied, creating a quarter-note/eighth-note combination. This approximates the feeling, but the nuances are often lost, as this rhythmic feel is closer to a shuffle rhythm than swung eighth notes (more on that later).

First, let's examine how the triplet undercurrent can be felt in a way that more accurately hints at the actual swing feel. Rather than assigning the phrase "tri-puh-let" to the figure, we use the syllables "doo-dle-la." This is derived from Clark Terry's instruction on doodle tonguing on the trumpet. Repeat the "doo-dle-la" syllables in time and then slightly shift the emphasis to the "la" syllable. This imparts the feeling of a pronounced upbeat, which is crucial to swing.

Next in the example, we've changed the notation to quarter/eighth pairs to further demonstrate the idea. The "dle" syllable is silent, or sounded in the throat, rather than pronounced. Again, add slightly more emphasis to the "la" syllable. You should start to hear what sounds like shuffle or swung eighth notes.

Example 1 wraps up with a demonstration of how we might see this notation written and how the earlier parts of the exercise can be applied to conventional notation.

EXAMPLE 1

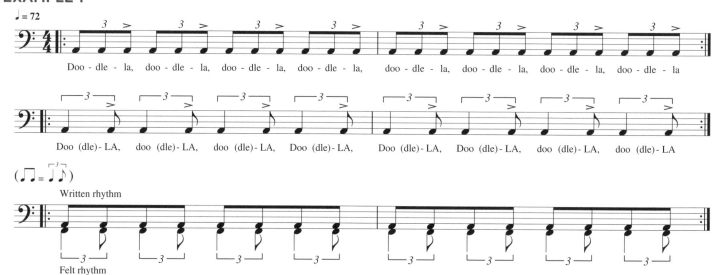

Walking bass lines can vary greatly in the kind of swing or shuffle rhythm played, depending on the individual musician and to the music of the moment. Here is an example in which the triplet undertone is clearly heard in the eighth notes.

EXAMPLE 2

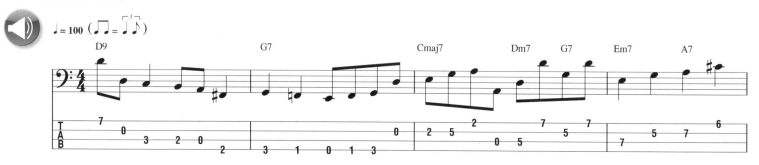

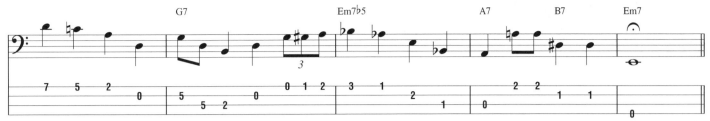

One clever idea I learned from an instructor of mine was to think of all the quarter notes in a walking line as beat 1. What this means is that you consider each note to have the intensity and forward motion that is usually applied to beat 1 of a new measure. The effect is understated but noticeable.

EXAMPLE 3

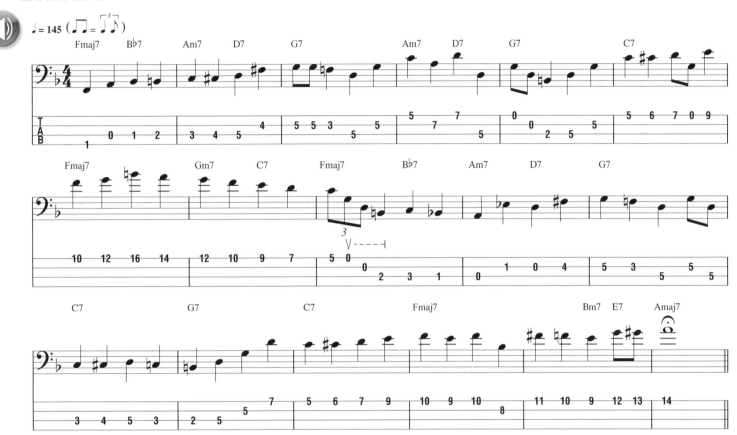

The priority of this "laying in the pocket" bass line is the relaxed intensity of helping to drive the band with the time feel, rather than choosing "hip" notes to impress the audience.

EXAMPLE 4

LESSON #50: BEAT MANIPULATION

In your listening, you've probably heard many examples of beat manipulation. Some players tend to play "on top" of the beat, while others play "behind" or right on the beat. Since we are constantly playing throughout a performance, we are also constantly negotiating the time feel between ourselves and the other musicians. It's important to have an awareness of divergent ways of playing the time, and successfully achieving awareness and control of our own placement of rhythm is fundamental to our job.

To review, take a look at the graphic below, which helps to visualize the different ways of playing. Each circle represents a unit of rhythm (e.g., a quarter note) on which we can identify three sections of each beat.

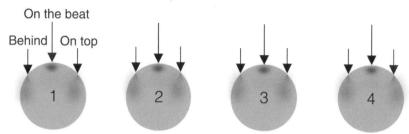

Each arrow represents the location where we would consistently place our attack in the context of an objective, metronomic standard. So, playing on the beat is to play precisely in time with the given beat. Playing on top of the beat is to play slightly in front of the given beat, and gives a sense of urgency or intensity. Playing behind the beat, or "laying back," evokes a more relaxed feeling.

Listen to these next examples, where my fantastic colleagues, Oscar Perez (piano) and Ulysses Owens Jr. (drums), and I demonstrate the three types of beat manipulation. First, we play behind the beat, then on the beat, and lastly, on top of the beat.

EXAMPLE 1

EXAMPLE 2

EXAMPLE 3

A really compelling way to use this rhythmic control is to place phrases or overall time feels against a contrasting feeling. In the examples below, you'll see phrases indicated with a "lay back" direction. These phrases *pull* against the time feel that is currently defining the excerpt.

EXAMPLE 4

EXAMPLE 5

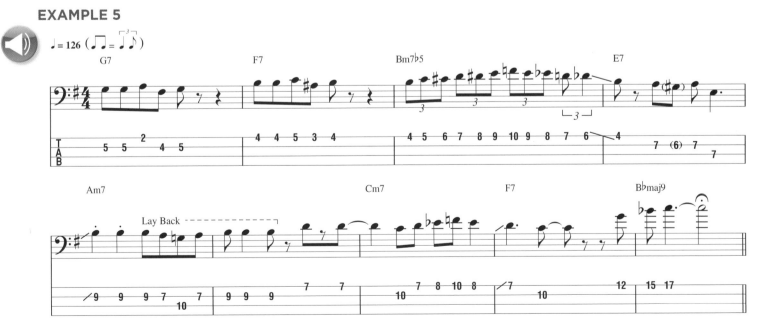

These examples are just a small sample of the ways in which we can use beat manipulation. Listen to the great musicians of yesterday and today and take special notice of where and how they control the beat. Mastering this skill takes time, but the effort is well worth the effort. Good luck!

ALL THE MAJORS

The fundamental components of jazz bass lines are chord tones. The core of most chords is comprised of three notes, collectively known as a triad. The major triad contains the root (R), the major 3rd (3), and the perfect 5th (5) of each major scale.

Let's take a look at the three main shapes of these triads.

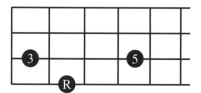
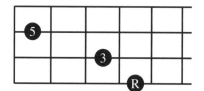
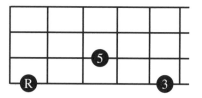

Take some time to play and memorize all 12 major triads through the cycle of 4ths.

EXAMPLE 1

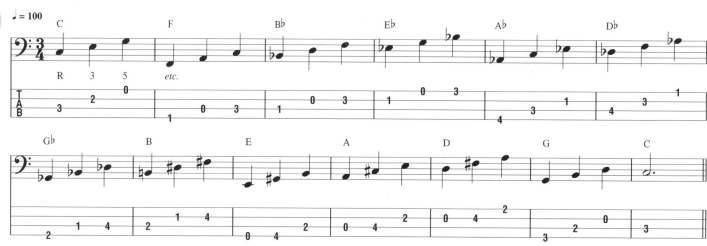

Now that you have played the major triads through the cycle of 4ths in 3/4 meter, try adding a fourth beat to each measure in the form of a chromatic approach note (A = Approach). Example 2 employs the chromatic approach note from below the root of the next chord (i.e., the lower-neighbor approach).

EXAMPLE 2

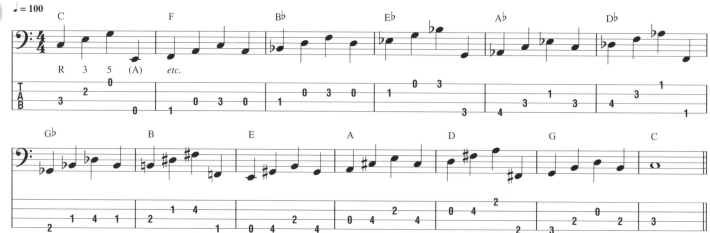

Example 3 employs the chromatic approach note from above the root of the next chord (the upper-neighbor approach). Sounds like walking bass to me.

EXAMPLE 3

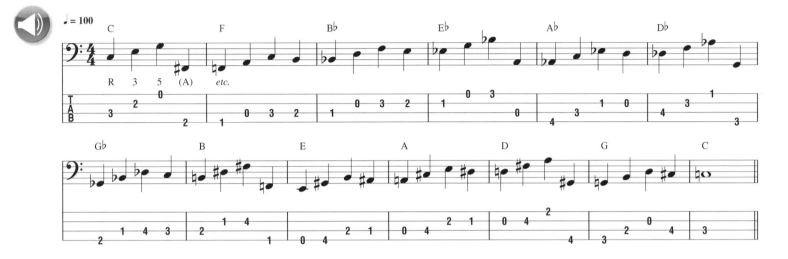

ALL THE MINORS

Minor chord arpeggios harbor minor triads at their core. The minor triad consists of the root (R), the minor 3rd (♭3), and the perfect 5th (5) of each natural minor scale.

Let's take a look at the two main shapes of these triads.

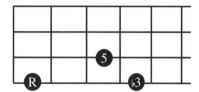 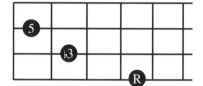

Take some time to play through all 12 minor triads through the cycle of 4ths.

EXAMPLE 1

Now that you've played the minor triads through the cycle of 4ths in 3/4 meter, try adding a fourth beat to each measure in the form of a chromatic approach note (A = Approach). Example 2 employs the chromatic approach note from below the root of the next chord (i.e., the lower-neighbor approach).

EXAMPLE 2

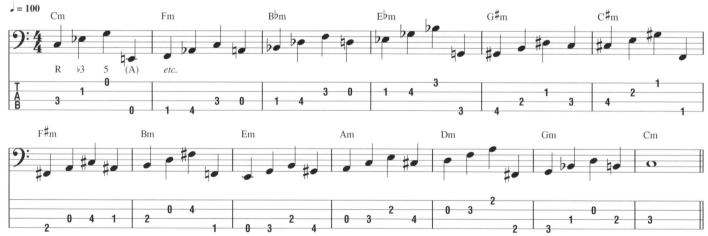

Example 3 employs the chromatic approach note from above the root of the next chord (the upper-neighbor approach). Sounds like walking bass to me.

EXAMPLE 3

LESSON #53: BOSSA NOVA BASS-ICS

The bossa nova feel is prevalent in jazz music, and every jazz bass player should know how to build a bossa nova bass line exclusively from chord symbols. The bulk of a bossa nova bass line is comprised of the root (R) and the 5th (5) of the chord being played. It is important to know whether to play a perfect 5th (5), a diminished 5th (♭5), or an augmented 5th (♯5). This can be determined by the chord's symbol.

Minor seventh and dominant seventh chords imply a perfect 5th. Here are three common perfect 5th shapes:

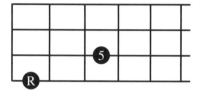 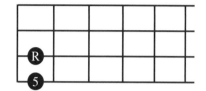 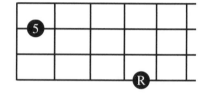

EXAMPLE 1

The half-diminished chord symbol (Bm7♭5 or B°7) implies a ♭5th. Here are two common shapes for playing diminished 5ths:

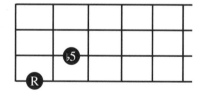 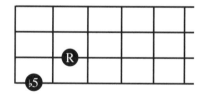

EXAMPLE 2

The augmented seventh chord (E7♯5) implies a ♯5th. Here are two common shapes for playing augmented 5ths:

EXAMPLE 3

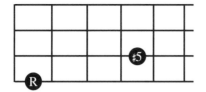

Let's look at an example of the bossa nova in action. It has a hypnotic dance rhythm that has made it one of the most popular "feels" in music. Can you spot the three different types of 5ths being employed? Would you be able to make up a part like this from the chord symbol alone? Notice the frequent use of a setup note on the last eighth note before a chord change.

EXAMPLE 4

LESSON #54: SKIPS

A wonderful addition to any walking bass line is the triplet skip. Adding skips to your walking will light up your lines with pizazz! You can place a skip on any of the beats in the measure. Let's take a look at the different ways we can use this exciting rhythm.

In these next four examples, the skip is isolated to one beat in each measure. You can add a skip to more than one beat in a measure, but it must be done with taste or it comes off as "busy."

EXAMPLE 1

EXAMPLE 2

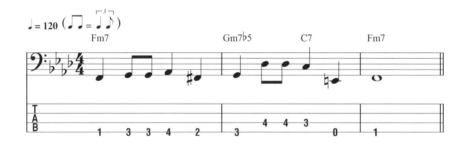

EXAMPLE 3

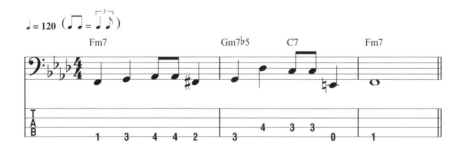

EXAMPLE 4

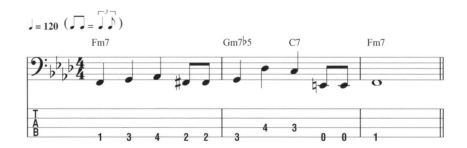

Let's have a bit of fun with skips in action. Notice that the skip appears on different beats in different measures, sometimes twice in a measure, and sometimes not at all. To help you make this technique feel comfortable under your fingers, the skips are being employed a lot more than in typical walking bass playing on a gig. Normally, you would balance out the use of skips with other exciting walking techniques, like triplets, slides, hammer-ons, ghost skips, and pull-offs.

EXAMPLE 5

LESSON #55: GHOST SKIPS

Ghost skips take the concept of the skip and make the short note a dead, or "ghost," note. Many people view this technique as the predecessor to funky dead notes. Ghost skips add interesting percussive rhythms to your walking lines. The ghost skip is achieved by firmly covering an open string with your fret-hand palm or fingers, without actually pressing the string all the way to the fingerboard, while simultaneously giving the string a firm pluck with the pluck hand.

EXAMPLE 1

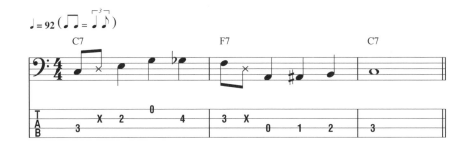

EXAMPLE 2

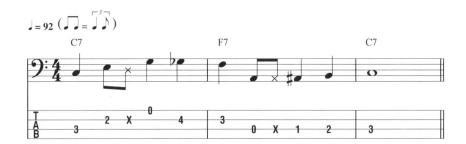

EXAMPLE 3

EXAMPLE 4

Enjoy playing through this example of the ghost skip in action. This jazz-blues in C gets an exciting boost by varying the rhythmic placement of these ghost skips.

EXAMPLE 5

LESSON #56: TRIPLETS

Triplets are a great way to add rhythmic and melodic intensity to your walking bass lines. There are a number of ways to achieve this; let's take a look at a few examples.

In this example, we use chord tones in the triplet on beat 1 of the first measure and scale tones in the triplet on beat 2 of the second measure.

EXAMPLE 1

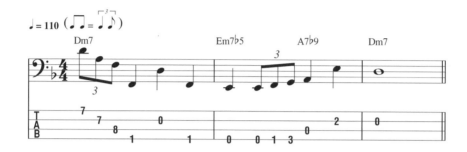

In this next example, note the use of the root, the 5th, and the octave root in the triplet at the end of the second measure. This note usage, coupled with the placement of the triplet on beat 4 of the measure, is a cool way to end a phrase.

EXAMPLE 2

Here, we rake the triplet with one finger to produce harmonics.

EXAMPLE 3

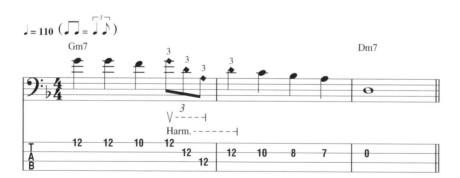

The triplet is an excellent technique to enhance a 16-bar minor blues. Normally, you would use a variety of walking techniques to enhance the line, but the focus here is on getting comfortable with triplets.

EXAMPLE 4

LESSON #57: SLIDES AND HAMMER-ONS

Slides and hammer-ons are very slick techniques that add pizzazz and elegance to walking bass lines. The slide is achieved by sliding a note up or down with the same finger, plucking the string only once.

Slides are excellent for approaching chord tones from below. You can slide from an open string, like we did here on beat 2 of the second measure, by plucking the open string and then sliding your first finger up a half step. Notice that we have placed the slide on a different beat in each measure.

EXAMPLE 1

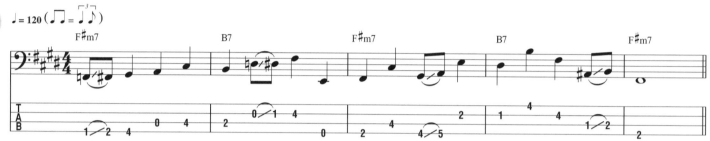

The hammer-on is achieved by placing one fret-hand finger on the fingerboard, plucking the string, and then hammering onto a note that is located above the initial note, on the same string. This next musical figure is identical to Example 1, but uses hammer-ons in place of slides. You can hammer on from an open string as well, like we did on beat 2 of the second measure.

EXAMPLE 2

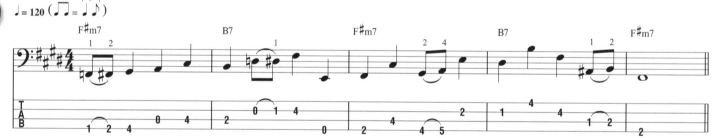

Here is a fun 16-bar progression that employs both slides and hammer-ons. Notice that the slide sometimes moves from a higher note to a lower note. Also notice that some of the slides and hammer-ons start on upbeats and end on the subsequent beats.

EXAMPLE 3

LESSON #58: PULL-OFFS

Pull-offs involve pulling your fret-hand finger from a higher, ringing note to a lower note. In walking bass, the pull-off requires plucking the second note with the fret-hand finger that is pulling off, to give it more clarity and power. Pull-offs are an amazing yet subtle technique to have in your arsenal.

Most pull-offs in walking lines end with an open note because they sustain better and are easy to pluck with the fret-hand finger. Pull the second note in each pair of slurred notes with one or more of your fret-hand fingers.

EXAMPLE 1

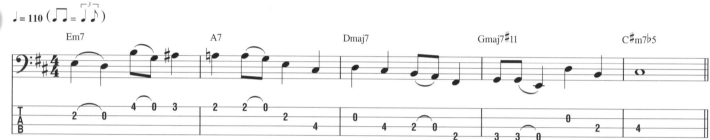

In this example, the pull-offs in the third measure end on fretted notes. This works well to create a subtle, low-intensity effect with the note, b ut it's much more difficult to produce an audible sound. This explains why it is rarely used in walking bass.

EXAMPLE 2

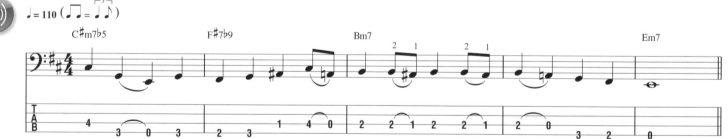

This 32-bar exercise is designed to help you gain facility with pull-offs. It's important to plan your shifts to "pull this off." Pay attention to the specified fingerings to help get you through the tricky passages. Each of the pull-offs requires a fret-handed pluck for the second note.

EXAMPLE 3

There are many ways to create harmonic interest in jazz walking bass lines. Many players get caught up in playing familiar-sounding patterns. One way that we can create more harmonic interest is to become familiar with inverted triads and how to connect them.

There are six possible triad inversions. If we add a chromatic approach note to beat 4 of a triad, we can set up the chord tone that we choose to place on beat 1 of the next measure. This first-beat note could be the root (R), the 3rd (3), or the 5th (5) of the new chord. Let's take a closer look at three ways to apply this concept to the most common and important jazz chord progression, the iim7–V7.

In this lesson, our progression cycles through six sets of iim7–V7s, which are bracketed for easy identification. Notice that this progression makes its way through the cycle of 4ths, the most common chord motion in jazz.

The chords in Example 1 are connected with basic root-position triads (R–3–5), with a chromatic approach note (A = Approach) leading into the root of each subsequent chord. While "easy on the ears," this basic inversion of the triad is both limiting for a soloist and a bit boring.

EXAMPLE 1

Here, the 3rd of each chord is placed on beat 1 of each measure. Notice that the chromatic approach note (A) on beat 4 of each measure leads into the 3rd of the subsequent chord.

EXAMPLE 2

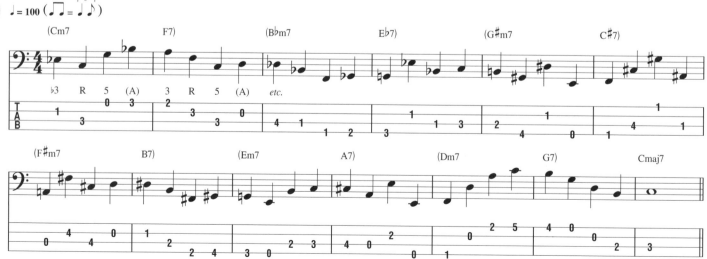

Here, the 5th of each chord is placed on beat 1 of each measure. Notice that the chromatic approach note (A) on beat 4 of each measure leads into the 5th of the subsequent chord.

EXAMPLE 3

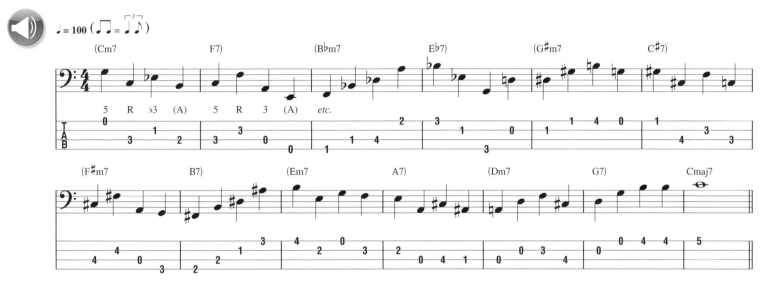

LESSON #60: A MAJOR PUZZLE

At first glance, we think of our major scale as a linear, seven-note string of notes. This assessment only scratches the surface. For example, there are seven different naturally occurring four-note chord arpeggios in every key of the major scale. If you play every other note of the scale, starting on each note, you will get these chord arpeggios (every key follows the same sequence):

Intervals of All Major Scales: R–2–3–4–5–6–7

G Major: G–A–B–C–D–E–F♯

ROMAN NUMERAL CHORD SYMBOLS FOR ALL KEYS	CHORD SYMBOLS (KEY OF G MAJOR)	SEVENTH CHORD ARPEGGIOS (KEY OF G MAJOR)
Imaj7 = One Major Seventh	Gmaj7	G–B–D–F♯
iim7 = Two Minor Seventh	Am7	A–C–E–G
iiim7 = Three Minor Seventh	Bm7	B–D–F♯–A
IVmaj7 = Four Major Seventh	Cmaj7	C–E–G–B
V7 = Five Dominant Seventh	D7	D–F♯–A–C
vim7 = Six Minor Seventh	Em7	E–G–B–D
viim7♭5 Seven Half Diminished	F♯m7♭5	F♯–A–C–E

Let's take a listen to this sequence as it lays out in the key of G in the lower positions of the bass.

EXAMPLE 1

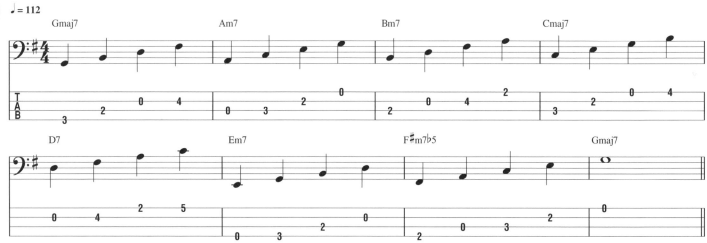

Notice the melodious nature of this progression of the seven four-note seventh chords in G major. Many jazz chord progressions are derived from combinations of these chords. All the major keys share the same chord sequence. This is why Roman numeral chord symbols are so useful. They represent the commonalities between all keys.

Here is a slightly more practical application of the seventh chords in G major, as applied to a 3/4 jazz bass line. The example is designed to illustrate how these chords work together to make a beautiful piece of music. Keep in mind that there are normally several key changes and chord alterations in jazz chord progressions. It was tempting to alter a few of the chords, but I wanted to keep all the chords diatonic (in the key) to the key of G major here. That said, the bass line employs chord tones, scale tones, and chromatic tones.

EXAMPLE 2

LESSON #61: MINOR FLIP

If you start and end a major scale on its sixth note, you get its relative minor scale. All 12 major keys have a relative minor key that has the same seven notes and chords as its relative major key. The only real difference is the sequence of the notes and chords.

KEY OF G MAJOR (FOUR-NOTE SEVENTH CHORDS)	KEY OF E MINOR (RELATIVE MINOR) (FOUR-NOTE SEVENTH CHORDS)
Gmaj7 = Imaj7	im7 = Em7
Am7 = iim7	iim7♭5 = F#m7♭5
Bm7 = iiim7	IIImaj7 = Gmaj7
Cmaj7 = IVmaj7	ivm7 = Am7
D7 = V7	vm7 = Bm7 (B7)
Em7 = vim7	VImaj7 = Cmaj7
F#m7♭5 = viim7♭5	VII7 = D7

Let's listen to how the seventh chords and arpeggios sound in the key of E minor when played sequentially in the lower positions of the bass.

EXAMPLE 1

While the minor key has all the same notes and all the same chords as its relative major key, it sounds very different and creates an entirely different mood in a musical phrase.

Here is a fun and practical application of the minor-key arpeggios, scale tones, and chromatics in a jazz walking bass line. Minor is very flexible and fun to play on bass. Normally, jazz chord progressions have several chord alterations and key changes. For this example, however, all the chords (except the B7) are diatonic (in the key) to the key of E minor.

EXAMPLE 2

LESSON #62: IONIAN MODE

Ionian is the name given to the first mode of our major-key modal system. If you start and end any of our 12 major scales on the first note of the scale, they will lay out as the Ionian mode. The common name for the Ionian mode is the major scale. You may know the Ionian mode as: Do–Re–Mi–Fa–Sol–La–Ti–Do.

Let's take a look at the Ionian mode and how the intervals lay out:

Ionian Mode: R–2–3–4–5–6–7–8 (R)

Here are a few common patterns of the Ionian mode as it lays out on the bass:

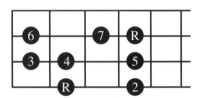 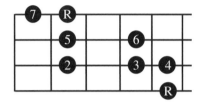 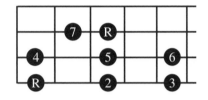

Here are the common chords that employ the Ionian mode when the chord appears as the first chord in a major-key progression or as the third chord in a minor-key progression. They are displayed as C chords, but we could have used any of the 12 notes for the symbol names:

CHORD SYMBOL	CHORD NAME	ARPEGGIO	INTERVALS
C	C Major	C–E–G	R–3–5
Cmaj7	C Major Seventh	C–E–G–B	R–3–5–7
Cmaj9	C Major Ninth	C–E–G–B–D	R–3–5–7–9*
C6	C Major Sixth	C–E–G–A	R–3–5–6
C6/9	C Six Nine	C–E–G–A–D	R–3–5–6–9*

*The 9th is simply the second degree (2nd) of the mode played above the octave.

Let's take a listen to the Ionian mode in action as it is played with its commonly used chords. Here, I have chosen to play melodic phrases so you can get a strong idea of the mode's color. The Ionian mode is used both in solos and in bass lines and has a very "inside" sound.

EXAMPLE 1

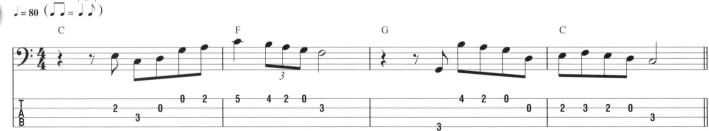

EXAMPLE 2

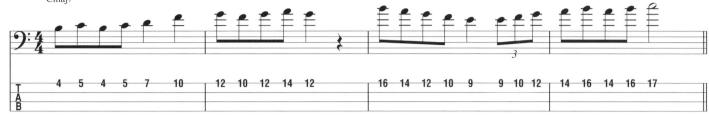

EXAMPLE 3

EXAMPLE 4

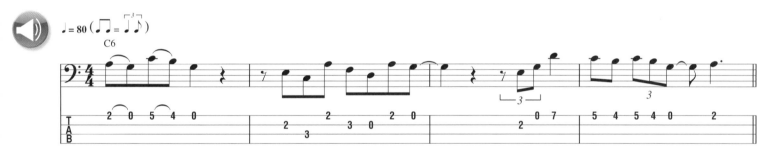

EXAMPLE 5

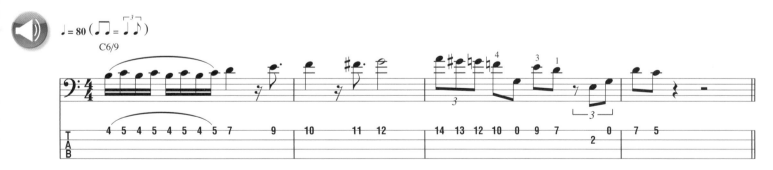

Dorian is the name given to the second mode of our major-key modal system. If you start and end any of our 12 major scales on the second note of the scale, they will lay out as the Dorian mode.

Let's take a look at the Dorian mode and how the intervals lay out:

Dorian Mode: R–2–♭3–4–5–6–♭7–8 (R)

Here are a couple of common patterns of the Dorian mode as it lays out on the bass:

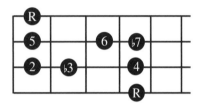
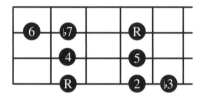

Here are the common chords that employ the Dorian mode when the chord appears as the second chord in a major-key progression or as the fourth chord in a minor-key progression. Additionally, Dorian is used with the first chord in a minor progression and in modal jazz vamps. The chords are displayed as D minor chords, but we could have used any of the 12 notes for the symbol names:

CHORD SYMBOL	CHORD NAME	ARPEGGIO	INTERVALS
Dm	D Minor	D–F–A	R–♭3–5
Dm7	D Minor Seventh	D–F–A–C	R–♭3–5–♭7
Dm9	D Minor Ninth	D–F–A–C–E	R–♭3–5–♭7–9*
Dm6	D Minor Sixth	D–F–A–B	R–♭3–5–6

*The 9th is simply the second degree (2nd) of the mode played above the octave.

Let's take a listen to the Dorian mode in action as it is played with its commonly used chords. The Dorian mode is used both in solos and in bass lines. The mode is usually employed when these chords are functioning as the second chord in a major chord progression, as the fourth chord in a minor chord progression, or as a substitute for the first chord in a minor progression. Additionally, it is an excellent mode for vamping on a single minor chord or in a modal jazz tune that employs very few chords. This affords the musicians an amazing amount of creative space.

EXAMPLE 1

EXAMPLE 2

EXAMPLE 3

EXAMPLE 4

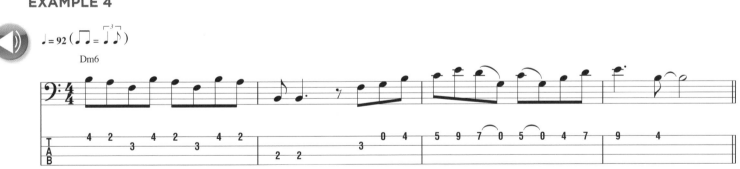

LESSON #64: PHRYGIAN MODE

Phrygian is the name given to the third mode of our major-key modal system. If you start and end any of our 12 major scales on the third note of the scale, they will lay out as the Phrygian mode.

Let's take a look at the Phrygian mode and how the intervals lay out:

Phrygian Mode: R–♭2–♭3–4–5–♭6–♭7–8 (R)

Here are a couple of common patterns of the Phrygian mode as it lays out on the bass:

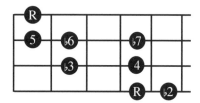 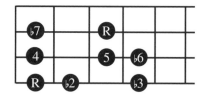

Here are the common chords that employ the Phrygian mode when the chord appears as the third chord in a major-key progression or as the fifth chord in a minor-key progression. When Phrygian is employed with the fifth chord in minor keys, the 3rd of the mode is almost always raised from a minor 3rd to a major 3rd. This creates the Phrygian dominant mode and the 7♭9 chord. This alteration is employed to strengthen the V chord in minor chord progressions. The chords are displayed here as E chords, but we could have used any of the 12 notes for the symbol names:

CHORD SYMBOL	CHORD NAME	ARPEGGIO	INTERVALS
Em	E Minor	E–G–B	R–♭3–5
Em7	E Minor Seventh	E–G–B–D	R–♭3–5–♭7
E7♭9	E Seven Flat Nine	E–G♯–B–D–F	R–3–5–♭7–♭9*

*The ♭9th is simply the second degree (2nd) of the mode played above the octave and lowered a half step.

In this example, the Phrygian mode is employed as a melody in a major progression.

EXAMPLE 1

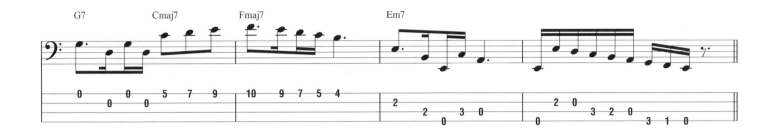

Here's the Phrygian dominant, or Spanish Phrygian, scale played against a B7♭9 chord. The major 3rd replaces the minor 3rd of the normal Phrygian mode.

EXAMPLE 2

Here's the Phrygian dominant scale being employed over a B7♭9 chord functioning as the V7 chord in the key of E minor. Listen to how the raised (major) 3rd provides color and suspense while setting up the Em7 chord.

EXAMPLE 3

Lydian is the name given to the fourth mode of our major-key modal system. If you start and end any of our 12 major scales on the fourth note of the scale, they will lay out as the Lydian mode.

Let's take a look at the Lydian mode and how the intervals lay out:

Lydian Mode: R–2–3–#4–5–6–7–8 (R)

Here are a couple of common patterns of the Lydian mode as it lays out on the bass:

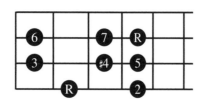 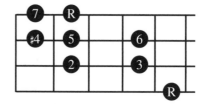

Here are the common chords that employ the Lydian mode when the chord appears as the fourth chord in a major-key progression or as the sixth chord in a minor-key progression. Lydian is also used with the first chord in major keys and with the third chord in minor keys. The chords are displayed here as F chords, but we could have used any of the 12 notes for the symbol names:

CHORD SYMBOL	CHORD NAME	ARPEGGIO	INTERVALS
F	F Major	F–A–C	R–3–5
Fmaj7	F Major Seventh	F–A–C–E	R–3–5–7
Fmaj7#11	F Major Seventh Sharp Eleven	F–A–C–E–B	R–3–5–7–#11*

*The #11th is simply the fourth degree (4th) of the mode played above the octave and raised a half step.

Here's how the Lydian mode sounds with the three chords that it compliments. To me, when the mode is isolated like this, it sounds like outer space—a very exotic but pleasing sound.

EXAMPLE 1

EXAMPLE 2

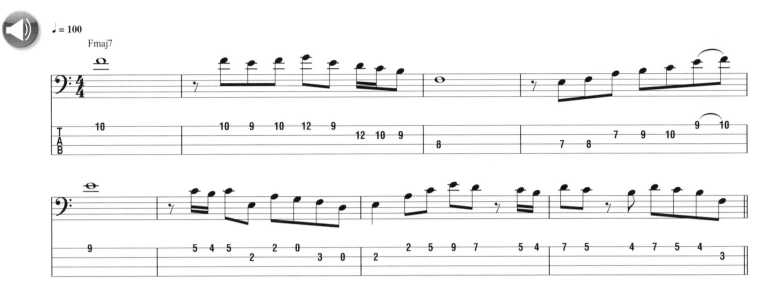

EXAMPLE 3

LESSON #66: MIXOLYDIAN MODE

Mixolydian is the name given to the fifth mode of our major-key modal system. If you start and end any of our 12 major scales on the fifth note of the scale, they will lay out as the Mixolydian mode.

Let's take a look at the Mixolydian mode and how the intervals lay out:

Mixolydian Mode: R–2–3–4–5–6–♭7–8 (R)

Here are a couple of common patterns of the Mixolydian mode as it lays out on the bass:

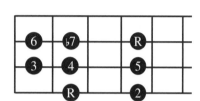 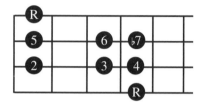

Here are the common chords that employ the Mixolydian mode when the chord appears as the fifth chord in a major-key progression or as the seventh chord in a minor-key progression. Mixolydian is also used with the first and fourth chord in major blues progressions. The chords are displayed here as G chords, but we could have used any of the 12 notes for the symbol names:

CHORD SYMBOL	CHORD NAME	ARPEGGIO	INTERVALS
G	G Major	G–B–D	R–3–5
G7	G Seventh	G–B–D–F	R–3–5–♭7
G9	G Ninth	G–B–D–F–A	R–3–5–♭7–9*
G7sus4	G Seventh Suspended Fourth	G–C–D–F	R–4–5–♭7

*The 9th is simply the second degree (2nd) of the mode played above the octave.

Here's how the Mixolydian mode sounds with three common chord types that it compliments well. Mixolydian often sounds unresolved (dominant) and, as a result, has a natural inclination to move towards the next chord in the progression.

Mixolydian goes with major blues progressions like bread and butter. Notice that we have three dominant seventh chords, each complimented by its respective Mixolydian mode and a few passing tones.

EXAMPLE 1

EXAMPLE 2

The suspended seventh chord has a moody, "open" sound and is often used in thematic modern jazz.

EXAMPLE 3

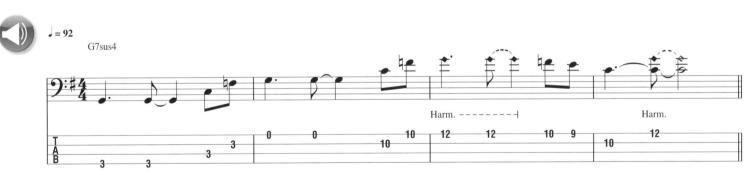

LESSON #67: AEOLIAN MODE

Aeolian is the name given to the sixth mode of our major-key modal system. If you start and end any of our 12 major scales on the sixth note of the scale, they will lay out as the Aeolian mode.

Let's take a look at the Aeolian mode and how the intervals lay out:

Aeolian Mode: R–2–♭3–4–5–♭6–♭7–8 (R)

Here are a couple of common patterns of the Aeolian mode as it lays out on the bass:

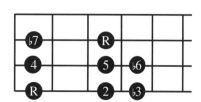 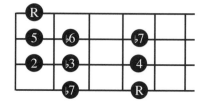

Here are the common chords that employ the Aeolian mode when the chord appears as the sixth chord in a major-key progression or as the first chord in a minor-key progression. Aeolian is the natural minor scale and represents the tonal center of our minor key. It was chosen to be the first mode in the minor key because the chords lay out in a very melodic way. The chords are displayed here as A minor chords, but we could have used any of the 12 notes for the symbol names:

CHORD SYMBOL	CHORD NAME	ARPEGGIO	INTERVALS
Am	A Minor	A–C–E	R–♭3–5
Am7	A Minor Seventh	A–C–E–G	R–♭3–5–♭7
Am9	A Minor Ninth	A–C–E–G–B	R–♭3–5–♭7–9*

*The 9th is simply the second degree (2nd) of the mode played above the octave.

The Aeolian mode is one of the most common sounds in Western music. Here, we will explore a few of the tonalities that the Aeolian mode finds itself at the center of.

Here is a walking vamp over a three-note minor chord functioning as the first chord in the key of A minor.

EXAMPLE 1

Here, the Aeolian mode is employed over an Am7 chord functioning as the sixth chord in the key of C major. This is a great and simple two-chord jazz progression for walking bass!

EXAMPLE 2

Here, the Aeolian mode is employed over an Am9 chord functioning as the first chord in the minor key of this traditional Cuban-style progression.

EXAMPLE 3

LESSON #68: LOCRIAN MODE

Locrian is the name given to the seventh mode of our major-key modal system. If you start and end any of our 12 major scales on the seventh note of the scale, they will lay out as the Locrian mode.

Let's take a look at the Locrian mode and how the intervals lay out:

Locrian Mode: R–♭2–♭3–4–♭5–♭6–♭7–8 (R)

Here are a couple of common patterns of the Locrian mode as it lays out on the bass:

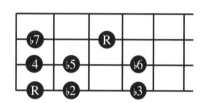 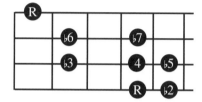

Locrian is generally employed with the chord that appears as the second chord in minor keys. The chord is displayed as Bm7♭5, but we could have used any of the 12 notes for the symbol name:

CHORD SYMBOL	CHORD NAME	ARPEGGIO	INTERVALS
Bm7♭5	B Minor Seventh Flat Five (B Half-diminished Seventh)	B–D–F–A	R–♭3–♭5–♭7

Here is a Locrian vamp. You don't hear this often, but it will give you a better idea of the Locrian mode's character when standing alone. This is a pretty dark and dissonant tonality.

EXAMPLE 1

Example 2 features Locrian (and the half-diminished chord it compliments) in its most likely musical situation—as the second chord in a minor key. This minor ii–V–i progression is one of the most popular phrases in jazz music.

EXAMPLE 2

Here is a quick series of ii–vs, another common usage of Locrian in Latin jazz.

EXAMPLE 3

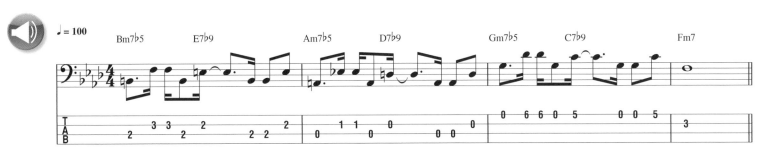

LESSON #69: MAJOR CHANGES

The diatonic major scale has seven notes and, as a result, harbors seven basic chords. Jazz music takes full advantage of these chords in the form of chord progressions, or chord "changes." The circular graph below represents the seven four-note (seventh) chords harbored in all 12 major keys. The uppercase Roman numerals indicate the major chords and their degree of the scale; the lowercase Roman numerals indicate minor chords and their degree in the scale. The m7♭5 symbol represents a half-diminished seventh chord. The chords in parentheses represent common chord substitutions for the naturally occurring chords.

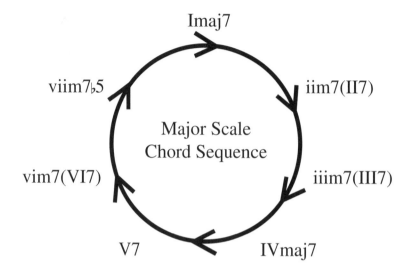

Let's explore some of the more common major chord changes used in jazz. Can you identify a similar progression in your favorite jazz standard from these examples? Notice that we have occasionally added a fifth note to our chords in the form of a 9th, 11th, or 13th as jazz musicians often do. Remember that the 9th is the 2nd played above the octave, the 11th is the 4th played above the octave, and the 13th is the 6th played above the octave.

EXAMPLE 1

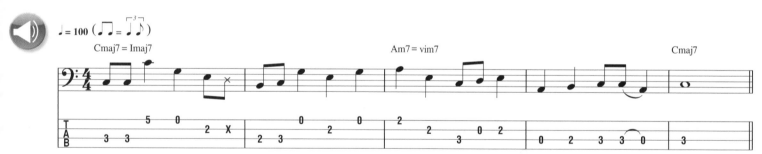

EXAMPLE 2

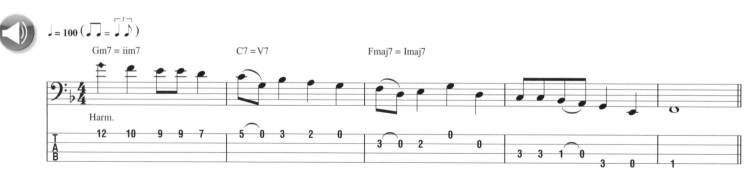

EXAMPLE 3

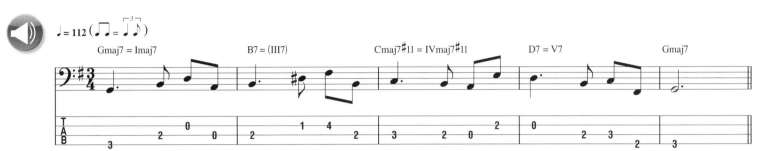

EXAMPLE 4

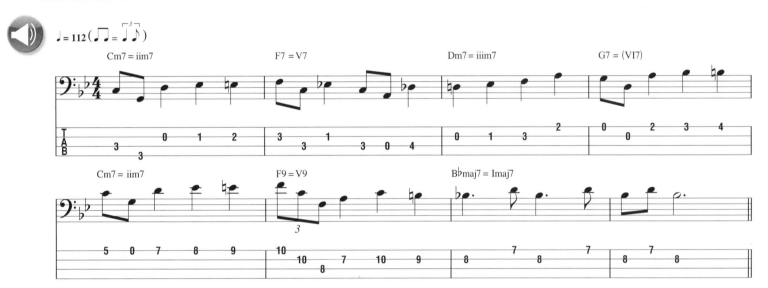

EXAMPLE 5

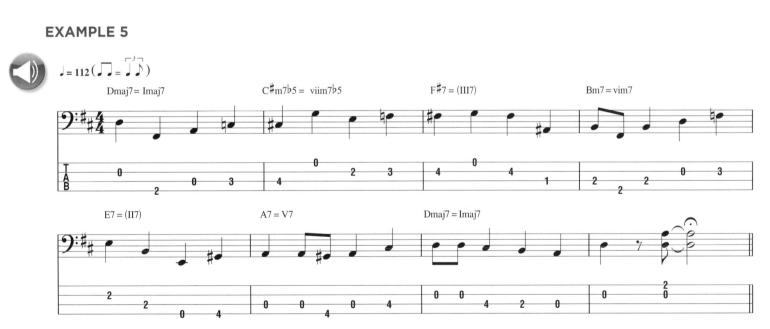

LESSON #70: MINOR CHANGES

The natural minor scale has seven notes and, as a result, harbors seven basic chords. Jazz music takes full advantage of these chords in the form of chord progressions, or chord "changes." The circular graph below represents the seven four-note (seventh) chords harbored in all 12 minor keys. The uppercase Roman numerals indicate the major chords and their degree of the scale; the lowercase Roman numerals indicate minor chords and their degree in the scale. The m7♭5 symbol represents a half-diminished seventh chord. The chords in parentheses represent common chord substitutions for the naturally occurring chords.

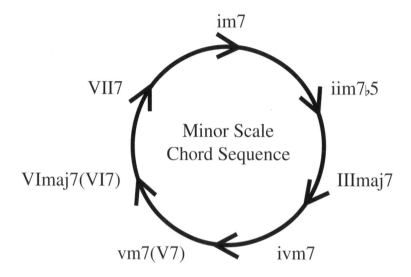

Let's explore some of the more common minor chord changes used in jazz. Can you identify a similar progression in your favorite jazz standard from these examples? Notice that we have occasionally added a fifth note to our chords in the form of a 9th, 11th, or 13th as jazz musicians often do. Remember that the 9th is the 2nd played above the octave, the 11th is the 4th played above the octave, and the 13th is the 6th played above the octave.

EXAMPLE 1

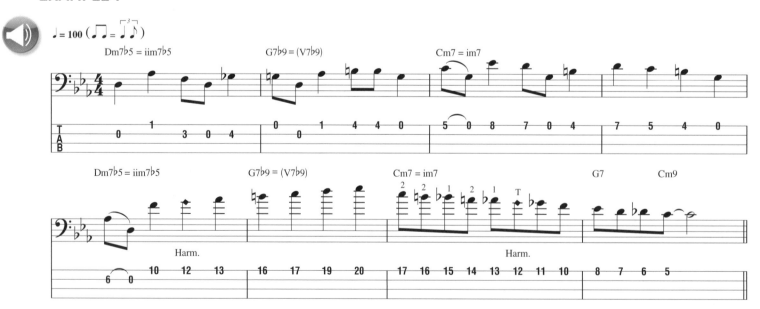

EXAMPLE 2

♩ = 105

EXAMPLE 3

♩ = 80

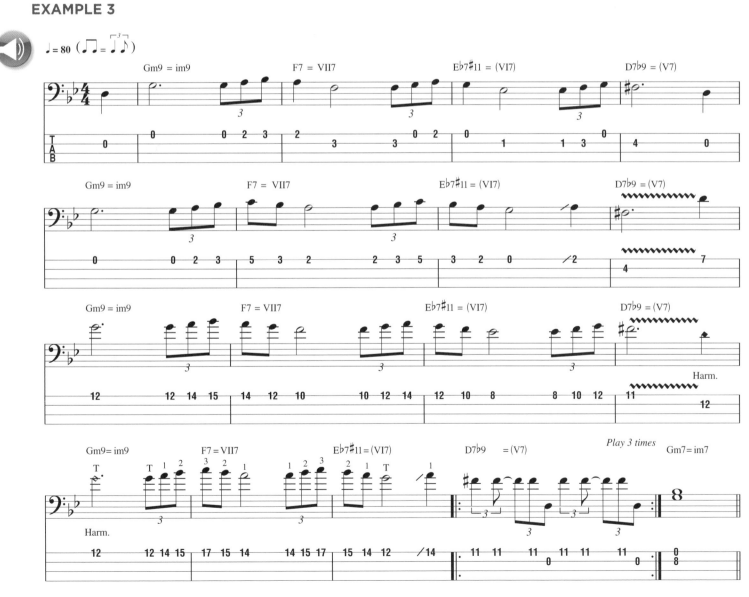

LESSON #71: LYDIAN DOMINANT

Lydian dominant is just that—a Lydian mode that is dominant. In order for a scale or chord to be dominant, it must have both a major 3rd and a minor 7th. If we lower the 7th of the Lydian mode by a half step, the Lydian dominant scale is created. Lydian dominant originates from its natural occurrence as the fourth mode of the melodic minor modal system. The 7#11 chord is harbored in the Lydian dominant scale.

EXAMPLE 1

C Melodic Minor (C-D-Eb-F-G-A-B)

♩ = 80

EXAMPLE 2

*F Lydian Dominant (F-G-A-B-C-D-Eb)

♩ = 80

*Fourth mode of C melodic minor

Lydian Dominant Scale

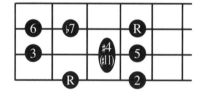

EXAMPLE 3

F7#11 Arpeggio (F-A-C-Eb-B)

♩ = 80

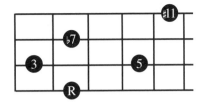

Here, Lydian dominant is used with G7#11 functioning as the V7 chord in a minor ii–V–i progression, it's most common usage.

EXAMPLE 4

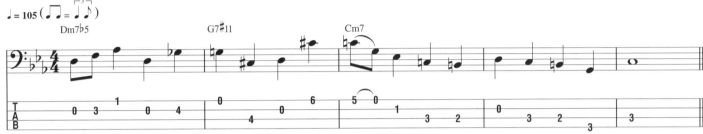

In this 16-bar jazz example, we see Lydian dominant employed with the 7#11 chord functioning as the V7 chord in measure 12 and 16 (G7#11), measure 6 (B♭7#11), and measure 10 (F7#11). We also see the 7#11 chord functioning as a tension-building chord in measures 11 and 14. Notice how the A♭7#11 chord in measure 11 and the F7#11 chord in measure 14 create a reflective pause in the music's mood.

EXAMPLE 5

LESSON #72: PHRYGIAN DOMINANT

In order for a scale or chord to be dominant, it must have both a major 3rd and a minor 7th. Phrygian dominant is the Phrygian mode with a raised 3rd. Phrygian dominant originates from its natural occurrence as the fifth mode of the harmonic minor modal system. The 7♭9 chord is harbored within the Phrygian dominant scale.

EXAMPLE 1

F Harmonic Minor (F-G-A♭-B♭-C-D♭-E)

♩ = 80

EXAMPLE 2

*C Phrygian Dominant (C-D♭-E-F-G-A♭-B♭)

♩ = 80

*Fifth mode of F harmonic minor

Phrygian Dominant Scale

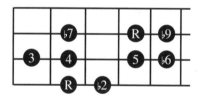

EXAMPLE 3

C7♭9 Arpeggio (C-E-G-B♭-D♭)

♩ = 80

7♭9 Arpeggio

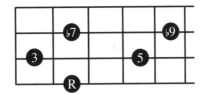

You can hear how dominant Phrygian dominant really is when employed with the V7♭9 chord. The C7 really wants to return to the im7 (Fm7) chord and achieve some resolution from its tension.

EXAMPLE 4

Here is an interesting little cycle of five sets of iim7♭5–V7♭9 progressions that resolve to D♭maj7. Although unlikely bedfellows, it works and you see jazz composers employ these progressions all the time. Phrygian dominant is just "major-sounding" enough to make it work.

EXAMPLE 5

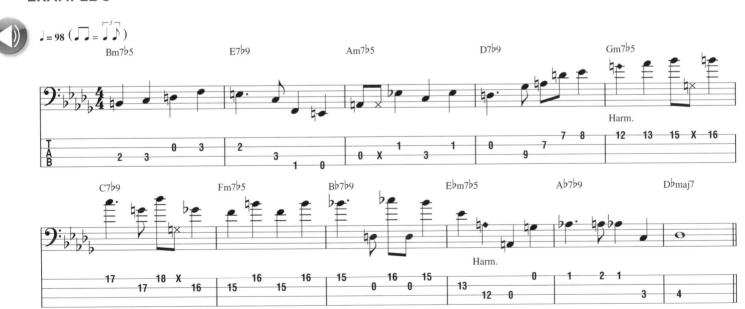

LESSON #73: HALF-WHOLE DIMINISHED SCALE

The half-whole diminished scale is a device used by jazz musicians over V7#9 and V7♭9 chords. It is a stand-alone scale with eight notes. The scale consists of four sets of alternating half and whole steps.

EXAMPLE 1

B Half-Whole Diminished Scale (B-C-D-D♯-E♯-F♯-G♯-A)

♩ = 80

Half-Whole Diminished Scale

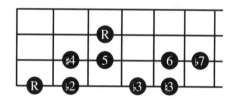

EXAMPLE 2

B7#9 Arpeggio (B-D♯-F♯-A-C𝄪)

♩ = 80

EXAMPLE 3

B7♭9 Arpeggio (B-D♯-F♯-A-C)

♩ = 80

7♭9/♯9 Arpeggio

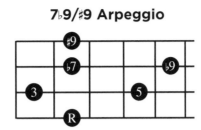

In these next two examples, we can become familiar with the tonality and fingerings required to truly begin to apply the half-whole diminished scale to our bass playing. Generally, you will see the chords employing the half-whole diminished scale come and go much faster than in these examples.

EXAMPLE 4

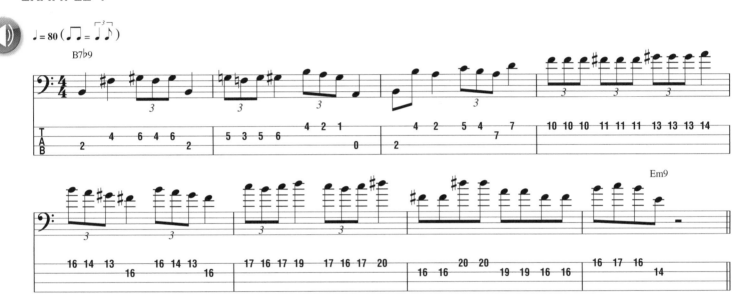

That one was hard to get out of.

This "stacking" of the 3rds of the half-whole diminished scale works really well with the V7♯9 chord. We find a crafty way to resolve this phrase. Notice the plain old E7 being employed to ease the transition to the Am7 chord.

EXAMPLE 5

LESSON #74: ALTERED SCALE

The altered scale and altered chords are a substitution option for V7 (dominant) chords. The altered scale is also occasionally used with half-diminished seventh chords. It is mostly employed in minor-key jazz phrases, but sometimes you will see an altered chord resolving to a major chord. The altered scale and its altered chords originate from the seventh mode of the melodic minor modal system. The altered sound lends interest to our normal harmony.

EXAMPLE 1

G Melodic Minor (G-A-Bb-C-D-E-F#)

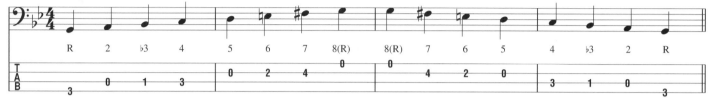

EXAMPLE 2

*F# Altered Scale (F#-G-A-Bb-C-D-E)

*Seventh mode of G melodic minor

Altered Scale

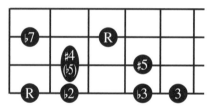

The altered scale is used with these altered dominant chords:

EXAMPLE 3

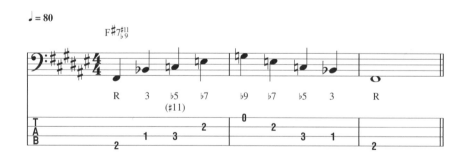

EXAMPLE 4

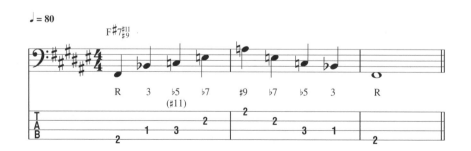

EXAMPLE 5

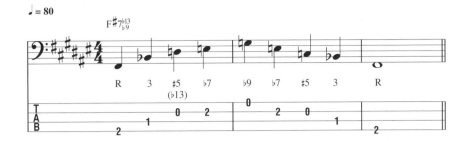

EXAMPLE 6

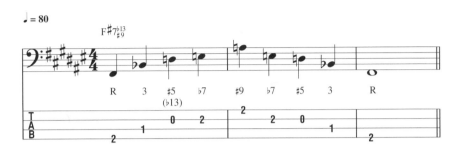

Altered Dominant Arpeggio

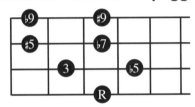

Half-Diminished Seventh Arpeggio

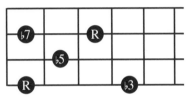

You can also play the altered scale with the half-diminished seventh chord:

EXAMPLE 7

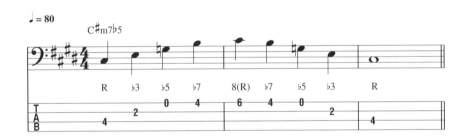

EXAMPLE 8

This little number is a fun way to get this "colorful" mode into your ears and under your fingers!

EXAMPLE 9

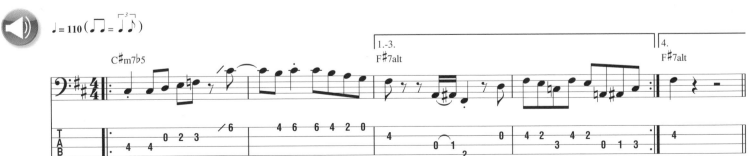

LESSON #75: WHOLE-TONE SCALE

The whole-tone scale is a six-note scale constructed from five whole steps (major 2nds), so six of our 12 keys contain the same notes, and the other six keys contain the other six notes. As a result, there are really only two whole-tone scales. The chords of the whole-tone scale become dominant sevenths with a ♯5th. The 7♯5 chord is usually used as a passing (V) chord in major and minor keys. It has also been successfully employed as the centerpiece of a few well-known jazz standards. The whole-tone scale has a perplexing sound.

EXAMPLE 1

*Whole-Tone Scale (A–B–C♯–D♯–F–G)
♩ = 80

*Any of the six tones can function as the root.

EXAMPLE 2

*Whole-Tone Scale (C–D–E–F♯–G♯–A♯)
♩ = 80

*Any of the six tones can function as the root.

Whole-Tone Scale

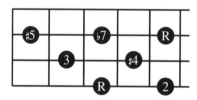

EXAMPLE 3

Notice the diagonal symmetry of the whole-tone scale as you run the arpeggios up the neck.

EXAMPLE 4

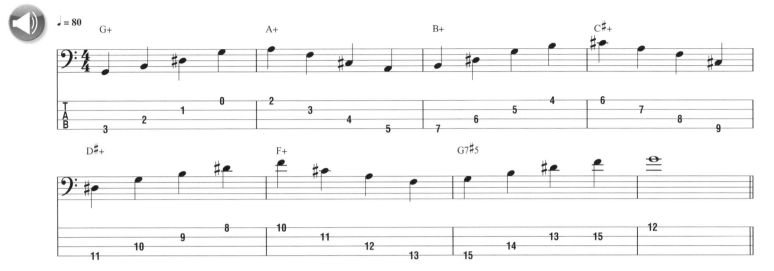

This little pattern is a neat way to move through the whole-tone scale, too.

EXAMPLE 5

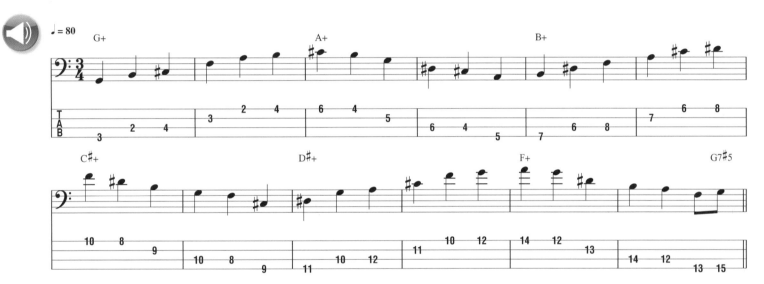

Here, the whole-tone scale is used over two V7#5 chords, one resolving to minor and the other resolving to major, one of its most practical uses.

EXAMPLE 6

LESSON #76: ii–V–I PROGRESSION

The ii–V–I progression is the most prevalent chord progression in jazz music. The chords progress as a cycle of 4ths, each chord is distinct, and when left unaltered, all come from the same key. This makes it easy for jazz composers to "ii–V" their way between chords, whether they share a key or not. Once you understand the power of the ii–V progression as setup chords for a chord a 4th away from the V chord, you will begin to understand jazz.

Here, Dm7 is being used as the iim7 chord in the key of C major.

EXAMPLE 1

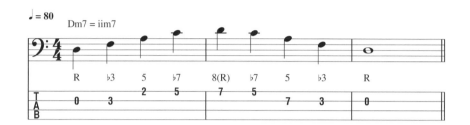

Here is D Dorian, the second mode of C major, a mode we can use with our Dm7 chord in C major.

EXAMPLE 2

Here is G7 being used as the V7 (dominant) chord in the key of C major.

EXAMPLE 3

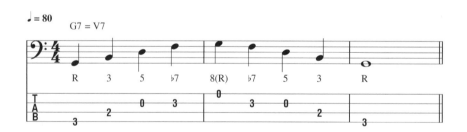

Here is G Mixolydian, the fifth mode of C major, a mode we can use with our G7 chord in C major.

EXAMPLE 4

Here, Cmaj7 is being used as the Imaj7 chord in the key of C major.

EXAMPLE 5

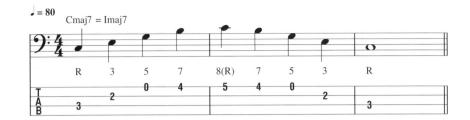

Here is C Ionian, the first mode of C major, a mode we can use with our Cmaj7 chord in C major.

EXAMPLE 6

Here are a couple of practical examples of the major ii–V–I progression in the key of C major.

EXAMPLE 7

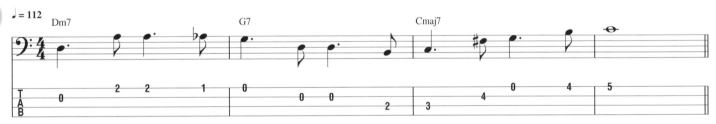

EXAMPLE 8

ii–V–i PROGRESSION

The minor ii–V–i progression adds a moody character to jazz music. It functions in a similar way to the major ii–V–I progression, in that both are generally setting up a chord a 4th away from the V chord. The ii–V–i should be another useful tool in your bass arsenal.

Here, Am7♭5 is being used as the iim7♭5 chord in the key of G minor.

EXAMPLE 1

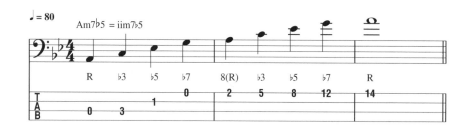

Here is A Locrian, the second mode of G minor, a mode we can use with our Am7♭5 chord in G minor.

EXAMPLE 2

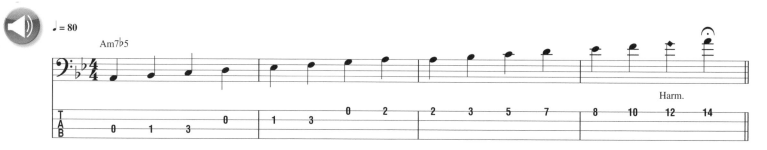

Here, D7♭9 is being used as the V7♭9 (dominant) chord in the key of G minor.

EXAMPLE 3

Here is D Phrygian dominant, the fifth mode of G harmonic minor, a mode we can use with our D7♭9 chord in G minor.

EXAMPLE 4

Here, we employ Gm7 as the im7 chord in the key of G minor.

EXAMPLE 5

Here is G Aeolian, the first mode of G minor, the mode we will expand our Gm7 chord with.

EXAMPLE 6

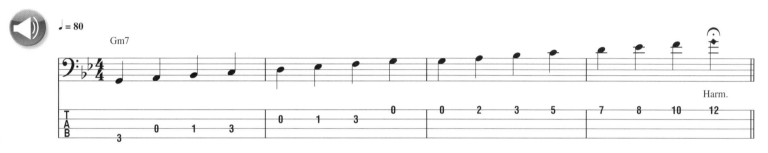

Let's put this minor ii–V–i progression to good use!

EXAMPLE 7

LESSON #78: SECONDARY DOMINANTS IN MAJOR KEYS

In the diagram below, the chords in parentheses represent common chord substitutions for the naturally occurring chords in major keys. Notice that every chord has a dominant substitute. We call these "secondary dominant" chords. All seven chords in each major key may be turned into a dominant chord with one alteration. In order for a chord to be dominant, it must have both a major 3rd and a minor 7th. The Imaj7 and IVmaj7 chords can be converted to dominant chords by lowering their 7ths a half step. The iim7, iiim7, and vim7 chords can be converted to dominant chords by raising their 3rds a half step. The viim7♭5 chord can be converted to a dominant chord by raising its 3rd a half step as well, even as the 5th remains flat (diminished). Secondary dominant chords are incredibly important to understand. Entire jazz styles have been defined by which chords of the major key are made dominant.

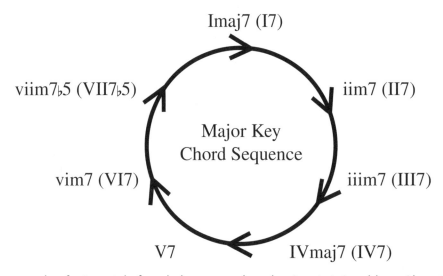

The most obvious example of a jazz style founded on secondary dominants is jazz-blues. Almost always, the I and IV chords are converted to dominants by lowering the 7th of each chord. Notice that the minor chords are sometimes made dominant by raising the 3rd, while others are left unaltered.

EXAMPLE 1

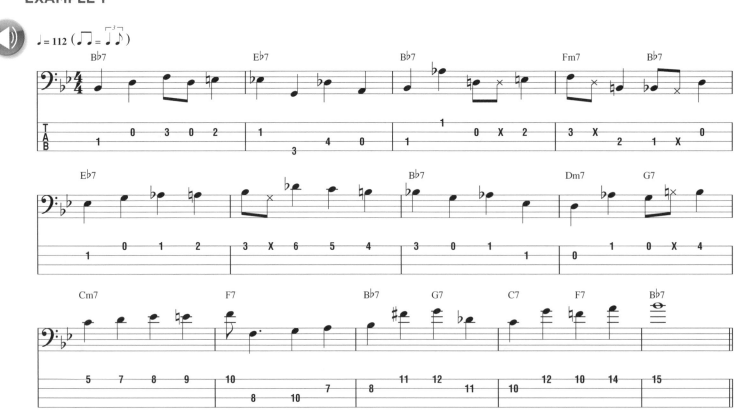

Here is an example of ragtime jazz. The I chord is left as a three-note triad with an implied major 7th, while the iim7, iiim7, and vim7 chords are all made dominant by raising their 3rds. Sounds a bit like a carnival.

EXAMPLE 2

LESSON #79: SECONDARY DOMINANTS IN MINOR KEYS

In the diagram below, the chords in parentheses represent common chord substitutions for the naturally occurring chords in minor keys. We call these "secondary dominant" chords. In order for a chord to be dominant, it must have both a major 3rd and a minor 7th. In minor keys, the vm7 chord is almost always converted into a secondary dominant by raising the 3rd of the chord a half step. The VImaj7 chord is frequently converted into a dominant chord by lowering the 7th of the chord a half step. Secondary dominant chords are incredibly important to understand. Entire jazz styles have been defined by which chords are made dominant.

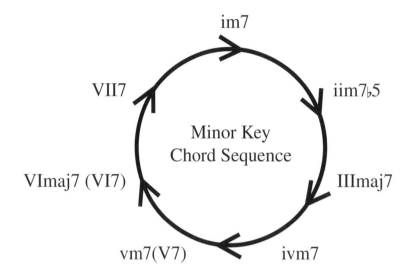

Here is a classic Im7–VII7–VI7–V7 minor jazz progression. Notice that all but the Am7 (im7) chord are dominant.

EXAMPLE 1

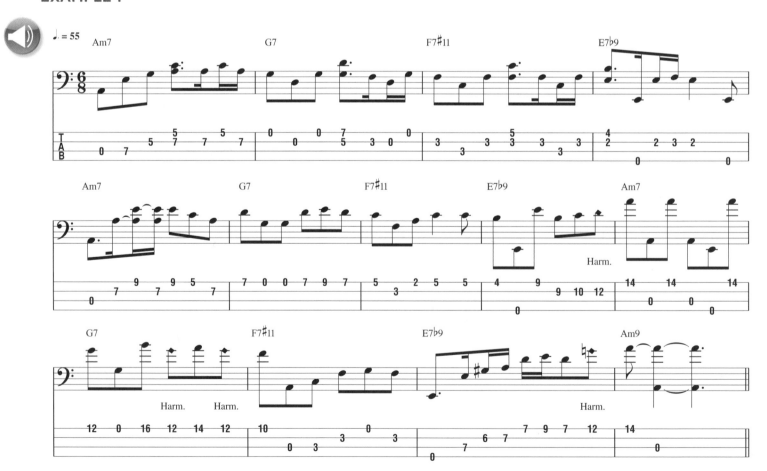

This example explores the most common secondary dominant usages in minor-key jazz: iim7♭5–V7, iim7♭5–V7–im7, and VI7–V7–im7. Can you spot them? Notice the use of a variety of dominant chords.

EXAMPLE 2

LESSON #80: MAJOR PENTATONIC SCALE

The major pentatonic scale is a great way to connect with your audience and draw them into your jazz playing. Its melodious nature serves as a nice contrast to your more "outside" lines. It can also be ornamented with chromaticism.

Major Pentatonic Scale: R–2–3–5–6

A Major Pentatonic: A–B–C♯–E–F♯

Here is an etude to familiarize yourself with A major pentatonic.

EXAMPLE 1

Here, we are still using the scale tones exclusively, but have added some jazz phrasing.

EXAMPLE 2

If you get comfortable playing "inside" the scale, you will naturally start to add chromatics and play a little "outside." Notice that Example 3 is a "jazzed up" version of Example 2.

EXAMPLE 3

LESSON #81: BLUES SCALE

The blues scale is another great way to connect with your audience and draw them into your jazz playing from the minor side of things. The ♭5th interval gives the scale its identity. Without it, the scale is simply minor pentatonic. Upon learning the blues scale, you can let the situation dictate whether you use the ♭5th (the "blue note"). The blue note adds a sassy flavor to your lines.

Blues Scale: R–♭3–4–♭5–5–♭7

A Blues Scale: A–C–D–E♭–E–G

Familiarize yourself with the A blues scale using these little jazz melodies, which happen to lay out very nicely on the bass! The blues scale is great for melodies and rhythmic solos over minor, dominant, or diminished chords.

EXAMPLE 1

EXAMPLE 2

Hear how the bass can really make a melodic statement in a jazz melody with the blues scale.

EXAMPLE 3

Here, we have a basic minor blues walking line that employs the A blues scale for most of it.

EXAMPLE 4

12-BAR MAJOR JAZZ-BLUES

The 12-bar major jazz-blues is the result of adding more harmony (chords) to the basic swing blues. This leads to several variations.

Normally, basic swing blues contains 12 bars and three dominant chords (I7, IV7, and V7):

EXAMPLE 1

In this next example, notice that we have added the iim7, iiim7, and VI7 chords to this normal jazz-blues, as well as a dominant I7–♭III7–II7–♭II7–I7 descending pattern in bars 11–13.

EXAMPLE 2

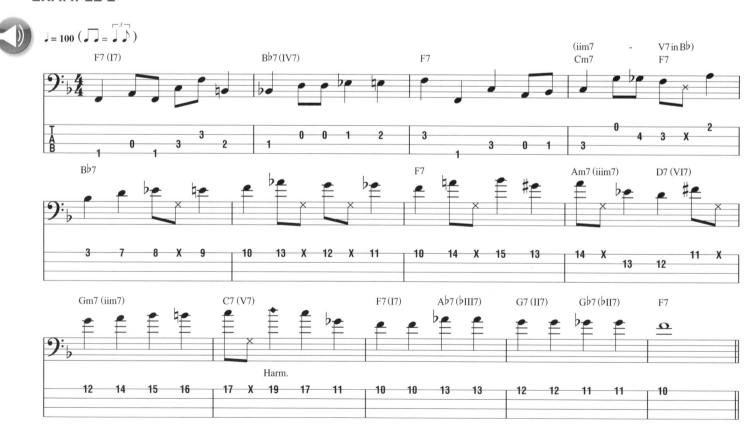

This jazz-blues makes use of a iim7–V7 setup in bars 3–4, a ♯iv°7 in bar 6, and chromatic dominants (tritone substitutions) in bars 8 and 10.

EXAMPLE 3

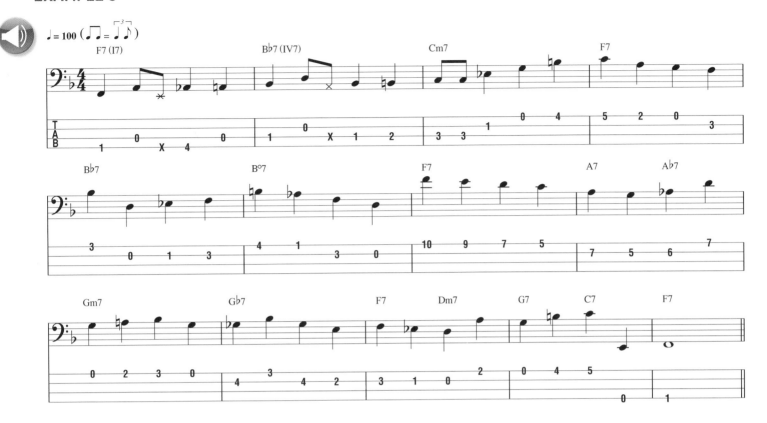

This jazz-blues makes use of the cycle of 4ths to move through the key of F with a series of diatonic and chromatic ii–Vs. Note the use of Fmaj7, the diatonic Imaj7 chord in the key.

EXAMPLE 4

12-BAR MINOR JAZZ-BLUES

The 12-bar minor jazz-blues is based on the im7, ivm7, and V7 chords of our minor harmony. Here is a basic example of the three chords at work.

EXAMPLE 1

In Example 2, we add the iim7♭5–V7 progression to bars 2 and 12 to create interest. We have also added the VI7 chord to bar 9, which employs Lydian dominant to start our turnaround. And don't miss the C7 setup chord in bar 4, which leads us to the Fm7 in bar 5.

EXAMPLE 2

In Example 3, we have employed a descending dominant chord pattern, im7–VII7–VI7–V7–♭V7♯5, in bars 1–4 to set up the Fm7 chord in bar 5. Notice the iim7–V7 setup in bar 8, which leads into our A♭7♯11 chord in bar 9, as well as the interesting note choices in bar 11—particularly the 9th of the chord (D) that opens the measure.

EXAMPLE 3

This flowing example employs the diatonic VImaj7♯11 chord in bar 9 to great, melodious effect and warrants the G7♯5 as a secondary dominant V chord in bar 10.

EXAMPLE 4

Here are a few examples of the 16-bar minor blues. The eight-bar phrases afford some great opportunities for jazz improvisation. The eight-bar phrasing likely comes from "old time" music, like Gypsy jazz and Irish fiddle music, which generally employ 16- and 32-bar forms comprised of two and four eight-bar phrases, respectively. The 16-bar minor blues has been employed extensively in Broadway show tunes, bebop, modern jazz, and popular music.

Here is a Gypsy jazz-style 16-bar blues. It is likely the origin of our American jazz-blues.

EXAMPLE 1

Example 2 is a modern jazz-style 16-bar minor blues adopted from a familiar show-tune form from the '40s. The basic form gives you the feeling that you are in a regular blues until you reach the turnaround (bar 12), which is a iim7–V7 leading to the relative major of the key (F) for only one measure, but then a minor ii–V leads us back into the minor key (Dm). These two choruses of the minor blues add several chord additions and substitutions. Notice the descending bass notes in bars 17–18 that introduce the second chorus of the blues. This progression sets up an opportunity for the VImaj7 chord to make an appearance in bar 19. All of the space in a minor blues affords these opportunities.

EXAMPLE 2

LESSON #85: 32-BAR (AABA) FORM

Here are some examples of the standard 32-bar form, the most common form in jazz. The eight-bar phrases of "old time" music remain, but the form is generally comprised of two eight-bar A sections with mostly the same chord progression, followed by one unique eight-bar B section, or bridge, followed by one more eight-bar A section with a chord progression similar to the other two A sections. These four eight-bar phrases give us the standard 32-measure jazz form. Be careful when improvising over this form, as it is easy to leave out an A section on the repeat because there are three A sections in a row if you count the last A (last eight bars) and the first two As (first two eight-bar phrases).

A Section 1 (8 Bars) = Verse or Theme

A Section 2 (8 Bars) = Verse or Theme

B Section (8 Bars) = Bridge

A Section 3 (8 Bars) = Verse or Theme

Here is a standard 32-bar jazz progression. The bass line represents what might occur under the melody the first time through the form, before the solos, which would be mostly straight walking. Notice that the bass line in the A section evolves with each new A section and that there is a slight chord alteration in bar 16 (second A section) to set up the bridge (B section).

EXAMPLE 1

LESSON #86: MODAL JAZZ

Modal jazz was developed by artists like Miles Davis in the '50s and '60s. Rather than using our standard diatonic chord changes as a framework for a tune, a mode is chosen as the tonal center. When a chord change occurs, the mode is usually transposed to a new key. Generally, modal jazz compositions have few chord changes. One chord may last up to 16 bars! This style of jazz affords the musicians an amazing amount of freedom when improvising due to the lack of fast-changing chords. Dorian and Mixolydian are two common modes to center a tune around.

Example 1 demonstrates a Mixolydian-style modal vamp. Only the turnaround uses a different mode. All that time on one chord affords the players the opportunity to superimpose a variety of improvisational techniques.

EXAMPLE 1

Modal jazz tunes centered on the Dorian mode afford an amazing amount of freedom. This 32-bar AABA form has only two chords! When playing with others, be careful not to go to the bridge too soon on the repeat. Notice how many "outside" notes this bass line gets away with—very indicative of the openness of modal jazz.

EXAMPLE 2

MINOR-MAJOR SEVENTH CHORD

The minor-major seventh chord is a great way to spice up minor chord progressions. It substitutes well as the im7 chord in minor keys. When it appears as the im7 chord, the minor-major seventh chord is derived from two different scales, harmonic minor and melodic minor.

Take a moment to play and hear the harmonic minor scale.

EXAMPLE 1

EXAMPLE 2

Minor-Major Seventh Arpeggio

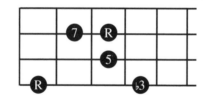

Here, C harmonic minor weaves its way through the three chords of a 12-bar blues, complementing our minor-major seventh chord.

EXAMPLE 3

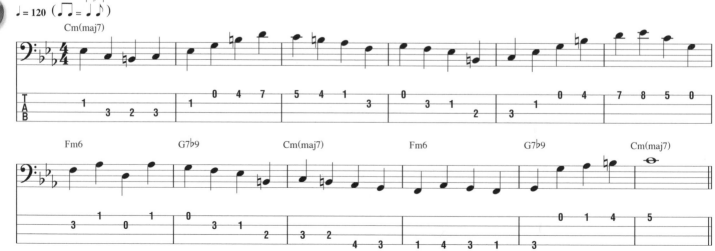

Take a moment to play and hear the melodic minor scale.

EXAMPLE 4

C Melodic Minor (C–D–E♭–F–G–A–B–C)

In this example, C melodic minor weaves its way through a 24-bar blues.

EXAMPLE 5

The diminished seventh arpeggio has a sinister sound on its own, but serves as an excellent passing and tension-building chord in jazz progressions. There are really only three diminished seventh arpeggios, with four inversions per arpeggio.

C°7	C–E♭–G♭–A	C♯°7	C♯–E–G–A♯	D°7	D–F–A♭–B
E♭°7	E♭–G♭–A–C	E°7	E–G–A♯–C♯	F°7	F–A♭–B–D
G♭°7	G♭–A–C–E♭	G°7	G–A♯–C♯–E	A♭°7	A♭–B–D–F
A°7	A–C–E♭–G♭	A♯°7	A♯–C♯–E–G	B°7	B–D–F–A♭

On the bass, there are two main shapes for the diminished seventh arpeggio. Notice that these arpeggios have a double-flat seventh, which is equivalent to a major 6th interval, and that they are constructed from three minor 3rds stacked on top of each other.

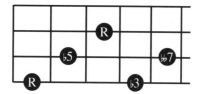 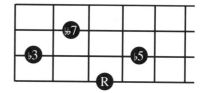

Notice that the diminished seventh arpeggios in Examples 1 and 2 contain the same notes.

EXAMPLE 1

EXAMPLE 2

In Example 3, we swing through four diminished seventh chords with the same notes. You can generally interchange them at will when you encounter any of the four.

EXAMPLE 3

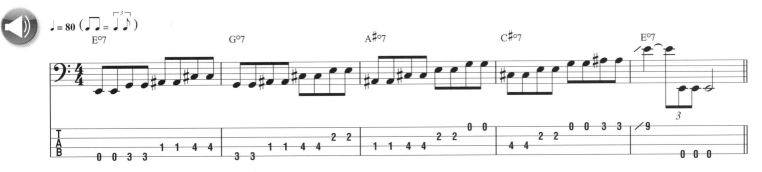

This bossa nova example illustrates how the diminished chord is often used in jazz chord progressions.

EXAMPLE 4

LESSON #89: DIMINISHED SCALE

The diminished scale, also known as the whole-half diminished scale, is the perfect scale to compliment the fully diminished seventh chord. The diminished scale is comprised of eight notes and alternates whole steps and half steps.

EXAMPLE 1

G Diminished Scale (G–A–B♭–C–D♭–D♯–E–F♯–G)

♩ = 80

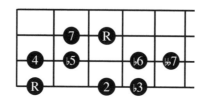

Diminished Scale

Here is the diminished scale for G°7, B♭°7, D♭°7, and E°7. This exercise is designed to get you swinging when you encounter one of these effective passing chords.

EXAMPLE 2

The diminished scale is most useful and colorful when you have time to explore it. In the following example, the diminished seventh chords last a full two measures! This gives the bassist enough time to consider a diminished scale line. Here, the progression uses diminished seventh chords to climb chromatically from the Imaj7 chord to the V7 chord before resolving.

EXAMPLE 3

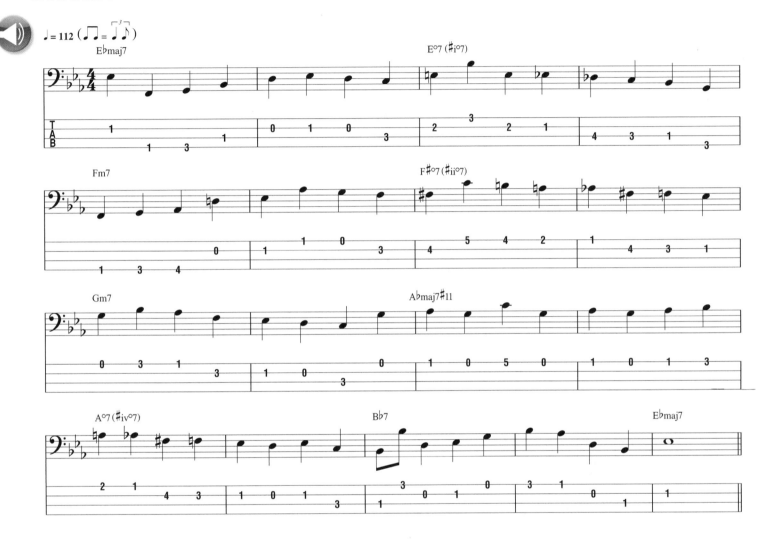

Check out this little diminished solo run so you can get used to making strong statements with diminished seventh chords.

EXAMPLE 4

LESSON #90: TRITONE SUBSTITUTION

Tritone substitution is one of the most poorly understood concepts in jazz. It is really quite a simple concept to understand and to apply to your bass playing. Tritone substitution takes one chord in a progression and replaces it with another chord that is a tritone (diminished 5th interval) away from the original chord. Sounds scary right? The good news is that it is almost always used to replace one dominant chord functioning as a V7 chord in the given chord progression with a ♭II7 chord. The result is a iim7–♭II7 progression instead of the usual iim7–V7 progression. Essentially, the chords move chromatically, instead of in 4ths.

Let's take a look at a typical iim7–V7–Imaj7 progression. Notice that this chord progression moves through the cycle of 4ths.

EXAMPLE 1

The tritone (♭5th) of the note C is G♭. To achieve tritone substitution, we simply replace the C7 chord with G♭7. You can see that we still get to the Fmaj7 chord, only chromatically instead of in 4ths.

EXAMPLE 2

Here, we have combined the two examples. Notice how the tritone substitution adds interest to an otherwise common progression. Jazz players are well aware of this.

EXAMPLE 3

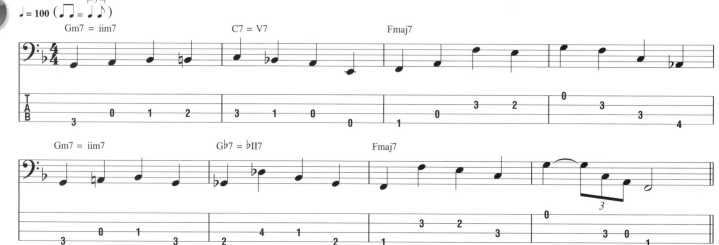

Enjoy this blues progression, which is riddled with tritone substitutions, indicated by an asterisk (*).

EXAMPLE 4

WALKING OUTSIDE

You can give your walking bass lines a lift by playing notes around or "outside" the chords and scale tones. This style of playing outside the chords is known as chromaticism. You can play any of the 12 notes in our Western system over most chords if you know what to play and where and when to play it. The trick is to continually check back in with the chord tones. This explains why most teachers suggest becoming a solid "inside" player before you attempt to step "outside" the chord and key structure. In many cases, it comes as a natural next step in the player's search for variety.

Here is a simple yet complete diatonic walking bass line. Familiarize yourself with this line so you can more easily digest the chromaticism that we will be adding.

EXAMPLE 1

This next example illustrates how easy it is to spice up a line by adding some chromatic notes that lead into the next chord. The trick is to know where you are and where you are going, sonically.

EXAMPLE 2

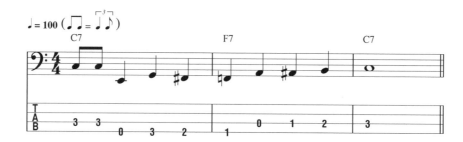

A good way to get comfortable with chromaticism is to "walk around" a chord. In this next example, notice that the chord tones are played on the strong beats (1 and 3) and the chromatic notes leading into them are played on the weak beats (2 and 4).

EXAMPLE 3

Here is a modal I7–IV7 progression. The progression is simplified for maximum study of chromaticism in walking. This line might be cool behind a sax solo. The chord tones are labeled between the notation and tab staves.

EXAMPLE 4

Here is an A minor blues that sounds pretty "out there" at times until you hear it with the chords played on piano or guitar, which holds it all together nicely. There is a lot of creativity available to the bassist who can walk outside.

EXAMPLE 5

LESSON #92: CHROMATICISM

Chromaticism can give your bossa nova bass lines zest. The key to using chromaticism is retaining the fundamental rhythm and harmonic integrity of the original bass line concept. Employing chromatic approach tones on the upbeats of beats 2 and 4 to set up the chord tones on beats 1 and 3 maintains the function of the line while giving it some spicy interest.

Here is a basic bossa nova bass line:

EXAMPLE 1

This next example maintains the same rhythm but replaces the eighth-note pickups with chromatic approach notes from below the chord tones. Notice how well this works.

EXAMPLE 2

Here, the approach notes come from above the chord tones. A slightly different effect, but it still works quite well.

EXAMPLE 3

Below are a number of chromatic-enhanced bossa nova bass lines. The chord tones are played on beats 1 and 3 of each measure, whereas the chromatic notes are played on the upbeats of beats 2 and 4. Keeping the strong beats (beats 1 and 3) as chord tones while consistently maintaining the bossa rhythm maintains the fundamental integrity of the line while the chromatic notes add color and interest.

EXAMPLE 4

JAZZING UP THE MELODY

Listen to and play the musical phrase below. It is modeled after a traditional jazz standard melody line. Notice that the phrase starts on the upbeat of beat 3. As a bassist, you are probably used to starting on the downbeat of beat 1. This is a chance to get comfortable with the freedom of space that solo upper-register instruments regularly enjoy as a result of being the likely one to play the melody.

Memorizing the melodies of jazz standards is an important first step to jazzing up a melody. Knowing a tune will take care of this approach to soloing, as you will discover that the ornamentation around the melody just "ought to be there" after you become familiar with, and tired of, the straight melody.

EXAMPLE 1

This next example maintains the integrity of the melody while adding triplet licks to key portions of the phrase. It is not unlike expanding a walking bass line. The main difference is the rhythmic phrasing.

EXAMPLE 2

Example 3 takes the phrasing "over the top," filling most of the space. That said, the melody is still intact. This might be a good way to play the last phrase of a jazzed-up melody for a crowd-pleasing climax.

EXAMPLE 3

Here, we take a minor melody through a similar evolution. Melody memorization and fluidity are the key components in preparation to jazz up a melody.

EXAMPLE 4

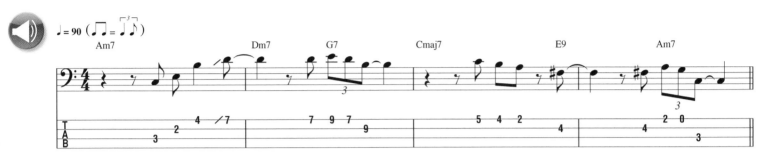

EXAMPLE 5

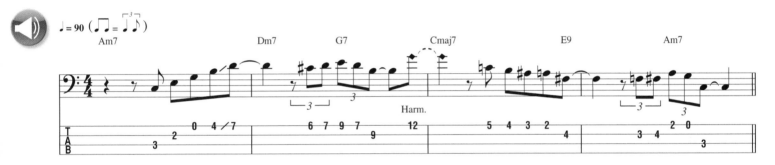

EXAMPLE 6

LESSON #94: SOLOING SHORTCUTS

Chromaticism is one of several great ways to enhance your bass solos. The key to using chromaticism is knowing where to land the run of notes. The best place to land is generally on a chord tone.

Here is a melodic phrase that uses G7 chord tones exclusively. Notice that this phrase already sounds pretty interesting due to the dynamic range of notes and the syncopated rhythms.

EXAMPLE 1

This next example adds chromatic triplets to measures 1 and 3 of the phrase. In an effective bass solo, it is a good idea to sometimes alternate "inside" and "outside" lines in order to keep your listeners engaged. Notice that the chromatic runs land on chord tones.

EXAMPLE 2

Here, the chromatic usage takes place in measure 3, which is bookended by nice inside playing in measures 1, 2, and 4.

EXAMPLE 3

This inside example, played over Cm7, employs a few scale tones in addition to the chord tones.

EXAMPLE 4

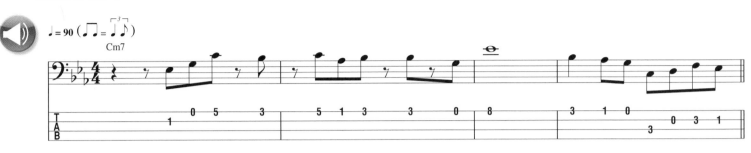

Notice that this chromatically enhanced phrase never uses the root of the chord.

EXAMPLE 5

Here is a iim7–V7–Imaj7 progression. Notice the chromatic approach to the 3rd of the F7 chord (from Cm7). In general, the chromaticism prevents this phrase from taking itself too seriously. The 4th of F7 is B♭, which is also the root of the B♭maj7 chord.

EXAMPLE 6

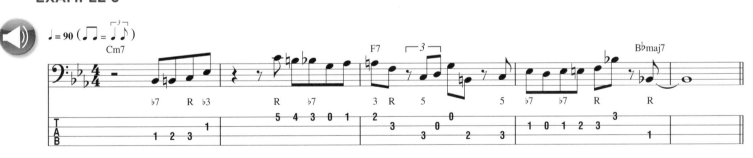

LESSON #95: BUILDING ON AN IDEA

Many bass students wonder how they can "break free" when walking over a modal vamp. This lesson will show you a few ways to lengthen your phrasing.

Example 1 is a standard eight-bar modal vamp over Dm6 employing the D Dorian mode. It returns to the root note (D) every two bars, on beat 1 of the measure. See if you can build two-bar phrases of your own that return to the root every two bars. Rhythmic techniques have been left out so that we can concentrate on phrasing. You can add walking techniques back in as you get more comfortable "feeling" the two bars.

EXAMPLE 1

Example 2 returns to the root note (D) every four bars, on beat 1 of the measure. See if you can build four-bar phrases of your own that return to the root every four bars.

EXAMPLE 2

Now that you are comfortable creating two- and four-bar phrases in your walking lines, try using the following template to create your own 32-bar modal walking bass line, being sure to target the few root notes that we have provided here. The rest is up to you. Use your Dorian modes for both chords and don't be afraid to add chromatic passing tones on beats 2 and 4 of a given measure, between chord and mode tones.

The audio example has piano and drums for you to play along with, with the few bass guide tones added for you to target.

EXAMPLE 3

A very fun and important part of playing traditional jazz is trading eights, fours, and twos. This means that each band member solos over a portion of the form and then hands off the soloing, or "trades," with another musician who responds with a solo of equal length. The drummer usually responds to each soloist with a rhythm break that is of equal length to the predetermined allotment of measures per trade, but not always. It is not unusual to trade 12 or 16 bars in jazz blues. In this lesson, however, we will focus on trading eights and fours over a 32-bar standard jazz form. First, we will look at soloing over eight bars each (trading eights). The piano will solo over the first eight bars while you walk, the drummer will take the second set of eight bars while you rest, and you, the bassist, will solo over the third set of eight bars. The drummer will answer you on the last eight bars before you all end on an F note. Normally, the trades happen after the solos and before the last playing of the melody, the "head out."

EXAMPLE 1

...musician playing four-bar phrases over the form. In this case, the order of the trades is ...ms, bass, and drums.

LESSON #97: BUILDING A SOLO

In this lesson, we will learn a few ways, of many, to build an effective jazz bass solo. This is not an easy task. The key components for an effective bass solo are phrasing, melody, and rhythm. It is important to be able to build your solo off notes other than the root note of the chord you are soloing over. It is also important to begin and end your rhythmic phrases in different places than our normal bass lines. We need to think like horn players and vocalists. Learning the melodies to the standards that you play is a great place to start getting acclimated to melodic phrasing.

In Example 1, we have mentally superimposed an Fmaj7#11 chord over our Dm7, as the former is built off the 3rd (F) of the latter. Starting the phrase on the 3rd gives us an immediate melodic boost. Additionally, we have employed the F Lydian mode. We are assuming that our Dm7 is a iim7 chord in the key of C major, which employs the D Dorian mode in a normal walking situation. F Lydian has the same notes as D Dorian, so, when we play F Lydian, we are simply moving the tonal center of the phrase to the 3rd of Dm7. Also notice the rhythmic variety at work here.

EXAMPLE 1

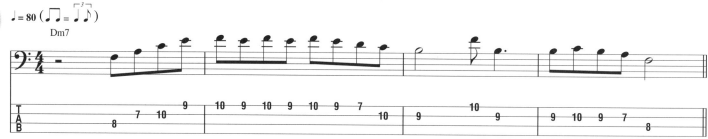

Let's employ these same concepts of superimposition and rhythmic variation to a G7 chord functioning as the V7 chord in the key of C major. Here, we will superimpose a Bm7♭5 chord and the B Locrian mode because they are the chord and mode built off the 3rd of G7 in the key of C major. G Mixolydian and B Locrian have the same notes. Again, we have simply shifted our tonal center to the 3rd of the G7 chord, B.

EXAMPLE 2

Now we will apply the same concepts to a Cmaj7 chord functioning as the Imaj7 chord in the key of C major. The chord built off the 3rd of Cmaj7 is Em7, and its respective mode is E Phrygian. Remember: moving our tonal center away from the root is a deliberate mental shift.

EXAMPLE 3

Let's combine these concepts in the form of a iim7–V7–Imaj7 progression in the key of C major. We will continue to employ superimposition and rhythmic variation, as well as add some chromaticism for tension. These concepts are a great way to make your solos more viable. Normally, you might not have this much time on each chord, but we need to stretch things out to become familiar with each chord.

EXAMPLE 4

LESSON #98: ARCO TECHNIQUE

You can really get your bass swinging with a bowed jazz solo or melody. Be warned that arco technique is a serious commitment for any string player, especially upright bass players. Be prepared to work carefully to develop a pleasant tone.

First, we will look at a few etudes to prepare you technically. Play closer to the tip of the bow than the frog, and begin with an up bow. Alternate bow direction as indicated. The up bow is the pushing direction of the bow; the down bow is a pulling motion.

In Example 1, we will explore swung eighth notes and slurred triplets.

EXAMPLE 1

You also need to make long bow strokes with vibrato on the long notes to warm them up.

EXAMPLE 2

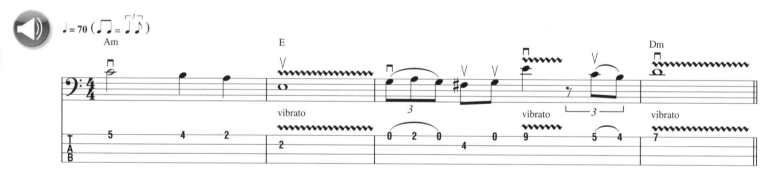

Here are some sweeping blues licks. Be sure to observe the slurs, and try different bowings.

EXAMPLE 3

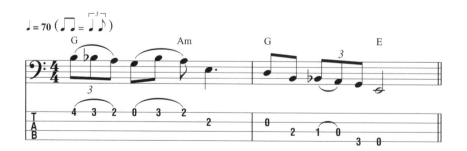

Bow solos sound best in a combo, but remember to be confident in your bow skills before attempting this in rehearsal or in public. It is a good idea to study classical bass, play the melodies to jazz standards, and play scales, arpeggios, and etudes with the bow often. Another good idea is to record yourself and hear what is really happening, as it is sometimes hard to judge what you are hearing from behind the bass. Bow markings have been excluded so you can try different bowings. Starting phrases on the up bow is a great way to get things swinging.

EXAMPLE 4

LESSON #99: RHYTHM CHANGES

Rhythm changes got its name from the chord changes to the song "I Got Rhythm." The form is a standard 32-bar AABA jazz form.

In this lesson, we will be exploring the original chord progression for this style. Many, many songs have used this form and chord progression as a template for creating original changes.

Example 1 displays the changes to a typical first A section.

EXAMPLE 1

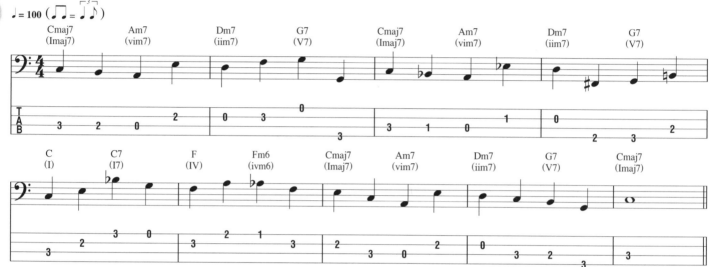

Example 2 displays the changes to a typical second A section.

EXAMPLE 2

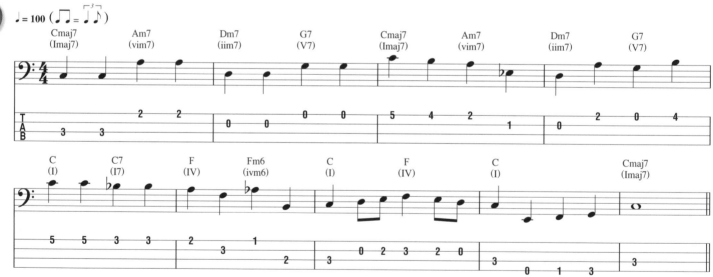

Here is the standard III7–VI7–II7–V7 bridge:

EXAMPLE 3

Here is the full, 32-bar AABA rhythm changes with a simple bass line so you can focus on the chord progression. Notice that we have added setup notes to the bridge.

EXAMPLE 4

LESSON #100: THREE-NOTE CHORDS

Let's take some time to look at a few easily "grab-able" chords, and chord sequences, on bass. The chords chosen here can work well both on your upright and on your electric bass. For the purpose of clarity, the sound samples are on electric bass.

A chord is two or more notes played simultaneously. The chords in this lesson are three-note versions. The first four chords have an A-note pedal as our bass note. They create a descending minor progression, which you will experience in Example 9.

EXAMPLE 1

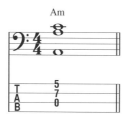

EXAMPLE 2

EXAMPLE 3

EXAMPLE 4

EXAMPLE 5

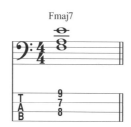

EXAMPLE 6

EXAMPLE 7

EXAMPLE 8

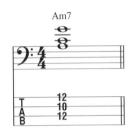

Enjoy playing this melodious bass-chord jazz-blues, which employs the chords we just studied.

EXAMPLE 9

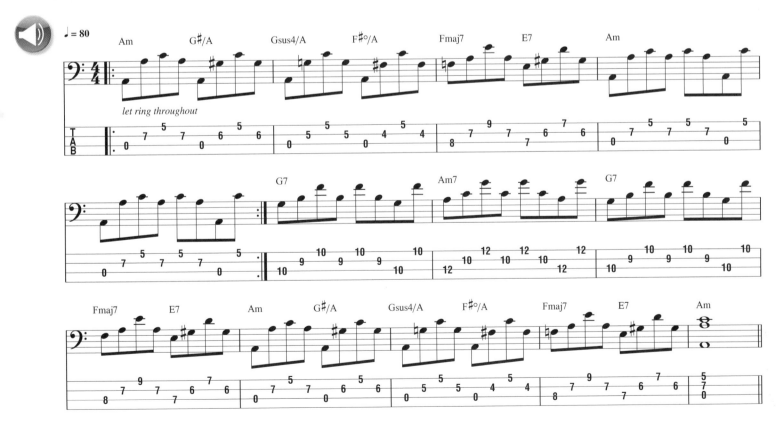

BASS BUILDERS

A series of technique book/CD packages created for the purposeful building and development of your chops. Each volume is written by an expert in that particular technique. And with the inclusion of audio, the added dimension of hearing exactly how to play particular grooves and techniques make these truly like private lessons.

BASS AEROBICS
by Jon Liebman
00696437 Book/CD Pack.................. $19.99

**BASS FITNESS –
AN EXERCISING HANDBOOK**
by Josquin des Prés
00660177.................. $10.99

BASS FOR BEGINNERS
by Glenn Letsch
00695099 Book/CD Pack.................. $19.95

BASS GROOVES
by Jon Liebman
00696028 Book/CD Pack.................. $19.99

BASS IMPROVISATION
by Ed Friedland
00695164 Book/CD Pack.................. $17.95

BLUES BASS
by Jon Liebman
00695235 Book/CD Pack.................. $19.95

BUILDING ROCK BASS LINES
by Ed Friedland
00695692 Book/CD Pack.................. $17.95

BUILDING WALKING BASS LINES
by Ed Friedland
00695008 Book/CD Pack.................. $19.99

**RON CARTER –
BUILDING JAZZ BASS LINES**
00841240 Book/CD Pack.................. $19.95

DICTIONARY OF BASS GROOVES
by Sean Malone
00695266 Book/CD Pack.................. $14.95

EXPANDING WALKING BASS LINES
by Ed Friedland
00695026 Book/CD Pack.................. $19.95

**FINGERBOARD HARMONY
FOR BASS**
by Gary Willis
00695043 Book/CD Pack.................. $17.95

FUNK BASS
by Jon Liebman
00699348 Book/CD Pack.................. $19.99

FUNK/FUSION BASS
by Jon Liebman
00696553 Book/CD Pack.................. $19.95

HIP-HOP BASS
by Josquin des Prés
00695589 Book/CD Pack.................. $14.95

JAZZ BASS
by Ed Friedland
00695084 Book/CD Pack.................. $17.95

**JERRY JEMMOTT –
BLUES AND RHYTHM &
BLUES BASS TECHNIQUE**
00695176 Book/CD Pack.................. $17.95

JUMP 'N' BLUES BASS
by Keith Rosier
00695292 Book/CD Pack.................. $16.95

**THE LOST ART OF
COUNTRY BASS**
by Keith Rosier
00695107 Book/CD Pack.................. $19.95

**PENTATONIC SCALES
FOR BASS**
by Ed Friedland
00696224 Book/CD Pack.................. $19.99

REGGAE BASS
by Ed Friedland
00695163 Book/CD Pack.................. $16.95

'70S FUNK & DISCO BASS
by Josquin des Prés
00695614 Book/CD Pack.................. $15.99

**SIMPLIFIED SIGHT-READING
FOR BASS**
by Josquin des Prés
00695085 Book/CD Pack.................. $17.95

6-STRING BASSICS
by David Gross
00695221 Book/CD Pack.................. $12.95

**WORLD BEAT GROOVES
FOR BASS**
by Tony Cimorosi
00695335 Book/CD Pack.................. $14.95

HAL•LEONARD®
CORPORATION

7777 W. BLUEMOUND RD. P.O. BOX 13819 MILWAUKEE, WI 53213

Visit Hal Leonard Online at **www.halleonard.com**

Prices, contents and availability subject to change without notice; All prices are listed in U.S. funds

0514